THE QUEEN
Observed

THE QUEEN
Observed

Edited by Trevor Grove

PAVILION
MICHAEL JOSEPH

First published in Great Britain in 1986
by Pavilion Books Limited
196 Shaftesbury Avenue, London WC2H 8JL
in association with Michael Joseph Limited
44 Bedford Square, London WC1B 3DP

Text © The Observer

Designer: Bernard Higton
Picture editor: Jenny de Gex
Picture researcher: Andrea Rittweiler
Observer picture consultant: Sue Cranmer
Caption writer: Moira Paterson

The Queen Observed
  1. Elizabeth II. *Queen of Great Britain*
  2. Great Britain – Kings and rulers – Biography
  I. The Observer
941.085'092'4   DA590

ISBN 1–85145–037–8

Printed and bound in Italy by Arnoldo Mondadori

CONTENTS

INTRODUCTION

No one has birthdays the way Queen Elizabeth II has birthdays. Aside from any other considerations, she is in the unique position of having two of them every year. The first, the actual anniversary of her birth, falls on 21 April. The second is her 'official' birthday—postponed until June in the hope of clement weather—when Her Majesty dons military garb, mounts a tall charger, jet planes buzz over the palace and the Colour is Trooped. More to the point, however, the Queen's birthdays are world occasions: there can scarcely be a corner of the globe where the event is not noted and celebrated, even if it is only in the form of cocktails at the Consulate. Film stars, writers, artists, statesmen may be honoured on a similar scale when they reach impressive milestones in their life's course. But the Queen, year in, year out, is more closely observed than any of them. She is, after all, the world's most famous woman.

This year, however, Elizabeth II is sixty, an anniversary deserving very special attention. If she were in a conventional job, she would be due to retire. Instead we honour a working woman who still seems to be in the full flood of her energies, devoted to her duties, still gathering and dispensing that serene brand of wisdom which Britain and even the world have come to associate with her reign ... and which remains, in most people's minds, one of the prime justifications for the monarchy today.

The Observer, the world's oldest Sunday newspaper, has chosen to produce this book partly as a tribute to the Queen; but partly also as a forthright journalistic enterprise, a reconsideration of the reality and role of the woman who in all likelihood still has 'long to reign over us'. For the fact remains that although millions of words and pictures and thousands of hours of airtime have been devoted to Queen Elizabeth from the very moment of her birth at 2.40 on a Wednesday morning in April 1926, she, the woman—wife, mother, grandmother, office worker, holiday-maker, race-goer—remains a very private person, a very public conundrum.

This book does not solve that conundrum. Instead it explores its facets, shining light on them from different directions and deliberately viewing the reflections through more than one pair of eyes and one photographer's lens. *The Observer* writers who feature here are not experts on the Royal Family. They are either columnists and feature writers who appear regularly in our newspaper and magazine pages, or specialists in quite other fields. Nor, in many cases, do these photographs come from the ranks of favourite court snappers. In other words, this book is not the product of spurious inside information: it is the product of trained eyes and thoughtful minds. It is not the Queen anatomized: it is the Queen observed.

Trevor Grove
Editor, *Observer Magazine*

Katharine Whitehorn
QUEEN OF HEARTS
─────The woman who wears the crown─────

The television lens allows little privacy for the royal expression. As Queen Elizabeth II sat in St Paul's Cathedral listening to the service for her jubilee in 1977, her face was sombre. Twenty-five years before things were different. The clouds of war and austerity were rolling back; there was a new world to build, or so it seemed, aglow with prosperity and social justice. Popular pundits talked about a new Elizabethan age and rather less popular pundits, who sneered at such things, seemed strangely out of step with the times. The Queen's marriage was new, her family young; the future must have seemed to glint ahead excitingly like a castle shining through early morning mist.

And what happened? The gradual dismantling of empire; the swinging sixties and the troubles of Princess Margaret; continuing irritating miseries about the state of the economy: this was not the lion that had saved the world roaring in grandeur, but a mangy old beast arguing with its keeper about the meat supply. Even the new brash utilitarian world we were supposed to be building seemed to have gone rusty at the edges, lying in the harshness of daylight like a disused factory site. Too much violence; too little honesty; Northern Ireland. No wonder she looked glum.

She was still looking grave as she left St Paul's and stepped 'out of God's blessing into the warm sun', and began, as monarchs before her had not done, to walk about among the crowds. Women split their faces into huge infatuated smiles; children waved little flags; men turned pink with pleasure, and one unfortunate failed to see her at all as he took a photograph of her instead. Slowly her expression relaxed and she began to look a little happier, then to light up; at the end of ten minutes she was positively grinning. Whatever promise the years had broken, this she had: these people wanted her, liked her, valued her. The reign was not a failure. The jubilee cameras said it all.

Now she is sixty; she has been ruling for thirty-four years. We will have the celebrations and the pictures again and she will look—well, radiant, what else do you say about the Queen? And once again we

At the Silver Jubilee service in St Paul's on 7 June 1977 (top left), the Queen looked sombre. By the time she came out with the Lord Mayor (top right) she seemed more cheerful, and when she joined the crowd in her walkabout (right) she looked positively radiant.

Bejewelled and girt with the orders of her office (right) Elizabeth II embodies her subjects' fantasies of royalty. In the sensible head-scarves she loves (below) she is also a reassuring image of ordinariness.

wonder what on earth it is that makes a queen a success, and what place a sovereign has at all in a supposedly modern and logical society. We shall go on trying, probably without much success, to sort out the difference between the monarch and the woman: a tricky enough task even if you are sorting the mogul from the man, the dancer from the girl above the ballet shoes. Asking now what she would have been like if she hadn't been queen seems as pointless as asking what Menuhin would have been like if he'd been tone deaf.

What you *can* ask is how much the set of monarchy as it is now is her own personal achievement; and what, indeed, she represents to the people who will buy a magazine in extra thousands if it has her face on the front. She is a female figurehead—but there are others. What makes her different from a First Lady, a Miss World or for that matter the Virgin Mary? (In the opinion of Robert Lacey, royal biographer, we have sneaked Mariolatry in again through the back door by giving such reverence to a queen.)

It isn't difficult to distinguish the Queen from Miss World or a pop heroine. Quite apart from not having to appear in body-hugging spangles, she doesn't die like a butterfly at the end of her hot short season and she has a far wider appeal. She's different, too, from a Jackie Kennedy or a Nancy Reagan, because their consort roles are set: they have no choice but to be charming and they're also temporary. They may not be politicians but they are certainly not outside and above the game like the Queen.

Elizabeth II's grasp on the national subconscious might well seem in line with a mother–goddess role—an astonishing 65 per cent of us apparently dream about her (including, so it is said, Alec Guinness and Judi Dench). Certainly the idea of an anointed monarch is quite irrational enough to get mixed up with religion. The Queen herself took her coronation to be a deeply religious experience, and had the Duchess of Norfolk do her rehearsing for her, up and down, over and over again, because it would have been sacrilegious to go through the motions herself. You certainly can't understand the monarchy (or most other

human institutions) unless you realize what an enormous amount of deep-down illogical sentiment goes into our most workaday actions; but goddesses don't have to go around opening hospitals and taking unkind criticism about their hats. A Sacred Person per se only has to *be*, but the Queen's own view is 'I have to be seen to be believed.'

Distinguishing the Queen from Mrs Thatcher is a rather different matter. Mrs Thatcher has the vote of the people and the Queen hasn't, but appointing prime ministers is about the only chunk of real power the Crown has left. The Queen had to exercise her judgement in appointing Alec Douglas-Home prime minister in 1963, probably wrongly, and about not appointing Heath in 1974, indubitably right. (She can take a hand, too, as she did when she talked Kenneth Kaunda into proceeding with the 1979 Commonwealth Conference.) Of her competence to wield such influence there can't, by now, be much doubt: she has read the 'boxes', the reports from government, for thirty years. Everywhere she goes they can be seen piled at airports following her around. She is the only person who has seen it all continuously for so long.

In a constitutional crisis or a hung parliament the power of the monarch might suddenly become very important indeed. And it's worth remembering that, although we have such a dread of a military takeover that our officers are scarcely allowed to wear their uniforms out of barracks, it is to the Crown that they owe their allegiance, not to Parliament. If an elected extremist faction tried to stop having elections, for example, the Queen could order the army to back her up in dissolving Parliament and trying for another.

Even this much power makes Elizabeth different from Princess Di or the Queen Mother. However muted, however residual, a monarch must have some power or she and her consort become, as Queen Victoria said disgustedly about Bertie and Alexandra, 'nothing but two puppets running about for show all day and all night'.

What do people see in the Queen? The delicious paradox, for those who go all misty eyed when they meet her, is that they think of her as a being from another world, but then are quite overcome when she turns out to be human after all. It can all become quite preposterous: if the Queen remarks that it's chilly for the time of year, onlookers note ecstatically that she talks just like a real person. Anyone who says anything disparaging about royals gets hate letters of a violence – and sometimes of a disgustingness – that makes one wonder if the senders are quite sane. Otherwise sensible people go around saying 'the Royal Family can't answer back' which, given that they have a well-equipped press office, a speech-making programme to make a Kissinger wilt and could well claim to be the first television monarchs, is plainly nonsense. The insight that tells the Royal Family it would be a mistake to answer back (a very different thing) is simply part of their shrewd perception of what best leaves their dignity intact.

But it's a mistake to write off people's apparently unhinged joy in their royalty as simply unreconstructed conservatism, a passion for tradition and the olde worlde akin to that which has them gawping their way round stately homes or bumping their heads on low beams at Stratford-upon-Avon. It's more interesting than that. Nobody is rational at the levels where old race memories twang, where ancient loyalties stir. And the feeling that anyone may have for belonging to one country or tribe and not another, for feeling 'this is my team, these are my people' exists as a deep territorial imperative—as the Falklands factor, which took most of the more rational analysts by surprise, obviously showed.

This feeling needs a permanent embodiment which no politician can supply. True, the odd charismatic leader like Churchill can occasionally inspire it, but it's a good deal easier to be moist eyed about an idealized family, to mix them up in a warm, subliminal way with feelings about childhood and Christmas and the olden days. It is a measure of the Queen's success that she has seemed to embody what the most ordinary among her subjects want—and one of the things they want is a certain amount of dignity, mystery even. Those who know her insist that she's extremely amusing in private (although you get marched off to the Tower if you repeat her remarks); it doesn't come out in any of her public utterances, because she doesn't think a jokey sovereign is what the people want.

Likewise some may think it would be splendid if the Queen chose different interests: smarter clothes, the opera, less mundane productions for command performances—but she knows better. You could say that horses and dogs are not exactly the preoccupation of most of her subjects either, but horses and dogs go with their *idea* of how royalty should carry on; opera they would view with dark suspicion.

Elizabeth succeeds not by being like them, but by being like their idea of what a queen should be. For of course her life is nothing like theirs. It's a quarter of a mile between her kitchens and her dining-room; if she wants to see a film she can do so in her own sixty-seat movie theatre; and while it's true that a string of racehorses may be normal for millionaires, it's not for the millions of citizens who warm to the awful headscarf and the sweet for the horses in the mackintosh pocket. Her skill in controlling her short-tempered dogs may be ordinary enough, but when once a dog got a pin in its paw at a dress fitting, Hardy Amies gave her a satin-covered magnet to pick it out with. The presents she gets beggar description: jewels, pictures, animals—including a pair of baby hippos, and a baby crocodile in a silver biscuit barrel which had to spend its nights in a long-suffering equerry's bath.

Except for something to put in the collection plate at Balmoral on Sunday mornings, she doesn't carry cash. Punctuality may be the courtesy of queens, but she doesn't exactly need Buckingham

Palace's 300 clocks. And in that palace alone the various flunkeys and functionaries number 200—it's been described as a government department set in a grand hotel—and most of them go around believing deeply in the mystique of monarchy. It is greatly to Elizabeth's credit that she can see past them to what is actually going on in the real world.

It's ironic that we all want to believe in the fantasy of the dream-queen, but coupled with an ordinariness with which we can identify. We want a queen who wears a gem-studded crown at one end and old bedroom slippers at the other; and it is for hitting this mixture for the most part dead right that this queen deserves congratulations. As Harold Nicolson said about Queen Victoria, 'her subjects could feel that in any crisis she was weeping the same salt tears into the same over-strong tea as they were'. Elizabeth has resisted all attempts to make her swing with the times: 'I'm not a film star', she said with contempt when Princess Anne wanted her to wear a mini-skirt. She's avoided, too, the arrogance of the aristocrat, which is more than can be said for her husband and her daughter, who has only now just made it back into the public's good books by way of her work for the Save the Children Fund.

The Queen embodies not the norm, but what Matthew Arnold called the Sunday-best morality of people: their idea of what a good woman with a good family ought to be like. She's at the top of a system of restraints that may have woefully broken down in your case or mine, but that must surely be going on *somewhere*—people want their sovereign to be better behaved, more restrained, more reliable in much the same sort of way that a parent is.

At least they do now. It can't be said that the monarchy has always been so determinedly respectable. George I arrived from Hanover with a couple of mistresses; some six English kings have been homosexual, though it rarely prevented them from propagating the royal line; the excesses of Queen Charlotte were dealt with by contemporary cartoonists in a way that would seem outrageous in our own day even for Mick Jagger; and the Prince Regent was not exactly the sort of role model of which your headmaster would approve, consoling himself even in old age with two massive middle-aged marchionesses.

When it comes to being a role-model of respectability, there's no denying that being a woman helps. The double standard works at the royal level as at any other: Elizabeth I, Anne and Victoria had to be above suspicion (if only to forestall any contamination of the royal line). When the rumours about Koo Stark were at their height, the Palace said of Prince Andrew: 'He is a young man of twenty-two—surely that speaks for itself.' They'd hardly have got away with the same implication about Princess Anne—had they ever thought of it.

Scandals are not only about sex, of course. They can be about money—look at all that unedifying fuss with Prince Bernhardt of the Netherlands and the Lockheed bribes. In this country the situation is not so much that it would be unthinkable for a consort to take bribes as that he would never have to anyway. The Queen is one of the richest women in the world and she could in fact finance the whole 'system', as the Royal Family calls it, out of her own pocket. But then, would the nation feel, perhaps, that it was nothing at all to do with them?

The squabbles about the Queen's money have to be seen in the context of her role as a parent figure. In themselves the sums aren't all that staggering—the whole circus costs less than half what the Royal Opera House in Covent Garden costs. And even if it were only an exercise in public relations it would still be a bargain at the price: what it does for tourism is one of the few bright spots on the balance-of-trade scene, and will go on being so. When asked why Americans should be so besotted with royalty after all their efforts to get rid of George III, one historian explained it neatly: 'It's the fairy stories that keep it going,' he said. 'Whoever heard of a girl kissing a frog and it turning into a handsome senator?'

So why do people get so upset at the cost of the royal train, at Prince Philip's civil list, at the idea of replacing the antique fleet of Andovers in which the royal person is perpetually borne aloft? For exactly the same reason, I suspect, that you rail at your mother's mink if you're suffering a cut in pocket money, however ancient the coat, however poor its resale value. It's *not fair*. If you don't want a monarchy at all and think it's an unjust system, that is an entirely respectable position; but it doesn't become more just or more desirable simply by being a little cheaper.

The Queen is a pro and she does the task well. Half a century ago, it might have seemed that there was practically no job left for a monarch to do. But our faith in the total rightness and strength of Parliament has declined. Several factors have contributed: the school-boy brouhaha of the institution as heard on radio, the dominance of a selected cabinet over Parliament as a whole; Lord Hailsham's dire warnings about an elective dictatorship, reminding us that we haven't got a written constitution; not to mention the evidence from so many ex-colonies that the Westminster system, far from being a rock to found nations upon, can be a sandcastle swept under by any high tide of political emotion. All this has made people uneasily aware that there's nothing God-ordained about the stability of our system, and the monarchy might be a lynch-pin that we would remove at our peril.

But the Throne has changed its relationship to the whole in a way that is none the less startling for being gradual. Just as the great landowners used to own houses because they were convenient places in which to live, and now spend nine-tenths of their time working to keep the homes themselves going in one way or another, so the monarchy, which used to run the country and had often to be restrained from running it for its own satisfaction, now seems to exist almost entirely for other people's benefit. As Daniel Counihan, for years the BBC court correspondent, said about George v: 'the power of the people was no longer something the monarch acquiesced in but something he embodied and defended.'

Even as late as Queen Victoria's reign the monarchy existed as the top of a pyramid of privilege that descended down through the lords and bishops, down through the Commons to the humble hat-doffers of democracy. It is only in this century that, despite the number of the Queen's friends who come from the older aristocracy, the monarchy has increasingly come to be seen as something to which the citizen relates—or doesn't bother to relate—directly. Witness the number of letters she gets where she is appealed to with confidence as the last resort in an intolerable case of oppression. If all power is a teeming heap of insects of one form or another, Her Majesty is no longer seen as the queen bee dictating the hive, but as something that you can see over the top of the ant heap, separate from all the creepy-crawlies that compose it.

If she sees being queen as a job, is there any likelihood that she will retire—will abdicate? Certainly the rule about never believing anything until it's officially denied applies no less to the Palace, which was busy indignantly rebutting any hint of romance within days of

Whether at home or abroad (here in Portugal, 1985) the Queen does her job to the satisfaction of most of her people: she is perceived as a good hardworking woman with a good family life.

Princess Anne's engagement. But it is probably about six to five against, for the time being anyway. The Queen always wished she had had longer herself to be a family woman before she was propelled on to the throne; she may want the same for Charles. Apparently she's anxious not to 'do an Edward VII' on him, but there seems little risk of that. Moreover there are things Prince Charles does well and with spirit that he could hardly do as a reigning monarch: being rude about architectural fashion, for example, or knocking the heads of doctors together to make them take alternative medicine seriously. (The involvement of *reigning* monarchs in fringe medicine has almost always been disastrous: look at Queen Juliana and her healers, at the Czarina and Rasputin. It would be a great shame if a posse of officers from the Guards should feel loyally obliged to poison, shoot and fling into the river the head of the holistic medicine movement.)

Besides, 'abdication' is a word with an ugly flavour in the Royal Family. You could say that many of the monarchy's current characteristics—emphasis on duty, lack of flamboyance or indiscretion, determination to do the job down to the last factory, town hall or water works—were shaped decisively by the events of 1936. For what went wrong that year was not just a simple matter of a royal passion for someone not deemed throneworthy; it went deeper than that. The boxes, those crucial instruments of power, were often left unopened or, worse, lying around Fort Belvedere for all to see; the Prime Minister had already stopped sending the King some of the more sensitive material long before the abdication, while MI5, alarmed by his links with Hitler, was actually keeping a file on him. The entire affair left Edward's successors with a strong feeling that being colourful was all very well, but that going over the top as he had done was not just unwise; it was an unforgivable dereliction of duty.

An abdication anyway must always send a weakening rumble through the foundations of the hereditary principle, even if another member of the family takes over (the pre-Conquest English kings were elected from among the ruling family, but it can't be said to have worked at all well). The point about hereditary office is that it avoids a lot of argument, and as arguments about thrones get conducted with blood and gunfire, the fewer there are the better. Henry v may have begged God before Agincourt not to punish him for 'the sins my father made in compassing the crown', but one of the key advantages that royals have over politicians is that they don't have to do anything to get where they are. As Jon Wynne-Tyson says, 'the wrong sort of people are always in power because they wouldn't be in power if they weren't the wrong sort of people'—which may be going a bit far. But it's important that there is somebody at the top who is immune from the sort of mud slung by those who are trying to *stop* a politician from becoming prime minister.

The other argument in favour of the theoretically absurd hereditary principle is that you are trained for it; you don't sudddenly do a Margaret Trudeau and flounce off, you know what the job entails. Queen Elizabeth has never had any doubts on this score—nor of the difference between what is private in her life and what is not. But this is the boundary along which there is the most friction. She's accessible, as few monarchs were before her father. But she can't bear the thought of having no life of her own, which is why the Fagan incident, when a man found his way into her bedroom at Buckingham Palace, upset her so much. One wonders how much of the poor security surrounding her was due to her devoted staff feeling that it was unthinkable anybody should break in—although Prince Philip, interestingly, thinks too much security positively provokes attack.

King Farouk once predicted that by the end of the century there would be only five royal families left: Spades, Diamonds, Hearts, Clubs and Windsor. The Scandinavian monarchies keep going, in their low-profile bicycling way, but most of the others have gone: to jetsetting, to exile, to that discreet old folks' home in the West Country said to exist for deposed royals alone. It is reasonable to wonder whether our own might have gone the same way, with a more wayward or flamboyant, a more tactless or a less dedicated character on the throne. The Queen can surely take credit for having done the job in the way that she thought it should be done: indefatigably touring the Commonwealth, keeping her dignity, staying in touch with a great part of the population, choosing a style that doesn't frighten people or repel them. Maybe the generation that adores David Bowie and Boy George doesn't think much about the monarchy one way or the other—but it's easy enough to envisage a scene where they'd decided that knocking the monarchy was as much a part of Being Young as being rude about the police.

In *1066 And All That*, Sellar and Yeatman have Warwick the Kingmaker setting a test-paper for sovereigns: 'Do you intend to be (a) a good king; (b) a bad king; (c) a weak king?' Even a good king, in our day, is apt to look weak, because he's simply not allowed to exercise that much power. And though he can be the glittering symbol at the top of a shiningly successful nation, it's a good deal harder for him not to seem, in a time of national difficulty, a sort of awful symbol of national impotence. A woman, though, can be an earth mother figure, like Mother Courage or the great Mom in *The Grapes of Wrath*, holding us all together, keeping us going, reassuring us that come what may the family will still endure. There is good in us yet, her patience implies: we will come through in the end. It's a fanciful image, of course. But we live by symbols; and successfully being a fanciful symbol is probably the most important job left for royalty today.

'I have to be seen to be believed,' the Queen has said. And seen she has been. Right after the Coronation she toured the country, meeting people at home (above, Glasgow, June 1953) and winning an affection that has grown steadily. Over the last 30 years she has developed into the ideal mother symbol: infinitely kind to children (right); presiding over our ceremonials in a family setting (top right, Trooping the Colour, 1984); and, above all, always remaining 'one of the people' (far right, 1976).

7

8

The Queen is an icon, serving the artist's purpose. She is idealized as Majesty – by Gunn (9) in 1954 and by Annigoni (5) in 1970; etherialized as pomp   by Birley (10) in 1948 and by Beaton (11) in 1960; elongated as dignity – by Mendoza (4) in 1982. Beaton (6) in 1968, Narraway (7) in 1971 and Madame Tussaud's (8) in 1983. She is made to fit the artist's idea of beauty – by Karsh (2) in 1967 and by Wallace (12) in 1972 – or of art – by Lederer (1) in 1936. Sometimes she is seen in military splendour – on Imperial by Cuneo (3) in 1962. And finally she is satirized – in *Spitting Image* (13) in 1985.

12

13

The royal image is used to sell practically anything. Coronation mugs were given away to schoolchildren, but the teatowels, tins of biscuits, ashtrays and penknives coined good reasons for traders to cheer the throne. Royal books are published and sold throughout the world to celebrate weddings, christenings, birthdays and jubilees and a royal magazine cover is a guaranteed boost to circulation.

7

8

The Queen is an icon, serving the artist's purpose. She is idealized as Majesty – by Gunn (9) in 1954 and by Annigoni (5) in 1970; etherialized as pomp – by Birley (10) in 1948 and by Beaton (11) in 1960; elongated as dignity – by Mendoza (4) in 1982, Beaton (6) in 1968, Narraway (7) in 1971 and Madame Tussaud's (8) in 1983. She is made to fit the artist's idea of beauty – by Karsh (2) in 1967 and by Wallace (12) in 1972 – or of art – by Lederer (1) in 1936. Sometimes she is seen in military splendour – on Imperial by Cuneo (3) in 1962. And finally she is satirized – in *Spitting Image* (13) in 1985.

12

13

The royal image is used to sell practically anything. Coronation mugs were given away to schoolchildren, but the teatowels, tins of biscuits, ashtrays and penknives coined good reasons for traders to cheer the throne. Royal books are published and sold throughout the world to celebrate weddings, christenings, birthdays and jubilees and a royal magazine cover is a guaranteed boost to circulation.

Tim Heald
A QUESTION OF UPBRINGING
The dutiful childhood of Princess Elizabeth

Serious historians don't much care for 'ifs' and 'buts'. However, for the rest of us what might have been is often as fascinating as what was. In the case of the Queen the ifs and buts triumphed over reasonable expectation. She was born in 1926 the daughter of a king's second son. The King had just turned sixty, the Prince of Wales was barely thirty years old. The probability was that George v would be succeeded by his eldest son who would, in turn, be succeeded by *his* eldest son. If that had happened Princess Elizabeth would now be a senior but relatively minor princess occupying much the same position in national life as her cousin Princess Alexandra: colonel-in-chief of the odd regiment, patron of the occasional charity; much loved but relatively peripheral.

That, surely, was the expectation when she was born. Yet from the first 'Lilibet' seems to have been doted on and expected of. Not just by her own parents, but more significantly by 'Grandpapa England'—bluff, Sealyham-loving George v—and his steelier spouse Queen Mary. 'I pray to God', George v is supposed to have said shortly before he died, 'that my eldest son will never marry and have children and that nothing will come between Bertie and Lilibet and the throne.'

Hindsight inevitably colours our perceptions but even the public seem to have had some sense that Elizabeth was destined for a more dramatic future than that of a minor royal. Newspapers and magazines headlined the birth, pouncing with an avidity that is still with us on a nice, upbeat, safe royal story to contrast with the depression of the serious news. It was the year of the General Strike and the foundation of the Hitler Youth. Not a lot to be optimistic about. Shortly afterwards, when her parents came back from a tour of Australia, they brought with them three tons of toys presented by the loyal subjects from down under.

That tour itself highlighted the peculiar style of her upbringing, which was formal even by the standards of aristocratic Britain of the

Riding with her uncle David — Edward, Prince of Wales — in 1933 (left), the seven-year-old Princess Elizabeth was assured of an important but relatively minor place in the royal pantheon. But when Edward abdicated in December 1936, her life was dramatically altered. She became heir presumptive — not apparent, a boy might still be born — and was subject to the image-building pressures prevalent at the time (right, Windsor, 1941).

The sturdy baby, nearly a year old (above), surveys the world with confidence from under her frills, and at the Bath Club swimming competitions (right, in June 1939) Princess Elizabeth's gaze is level and unafraid. Was it official photographers who created the story of her shyness?

day. Princess Elizabeth was less than a year old when her parents were sent off on the battle cruiser *Renown* for six months. There was a public farewell at Victoria Station, then three months with her Bowes-Lyon grandparents followed by three with her Windsor ones. The King noted her arrival in his diary and remarked that she 'came to see us after tea'. When her parents returned, the Royal Family all went out on to the balcony of Buckingham Palace to show themselves to the cheering crowd. Later, when they repaired to their own home, their first permanent one, at 145 Piccadilly, this ritual was repeated on the balcony there.

This is not to suggest that her parents were other than doting; they seem—against the odds—to have been a very close and loving family. But parents, especially royal ones, did not bring up their children in the way that most people now do. That job was, if not delegated to, at least shared with nurse, nanny and governess.

Elizabeth's first nanny was Clara Knight, known to the family as Alla and occasionally photographed looking rather overdressed with some dead animal round her neck and a felt hat with a brim pulled well down over the ears. She looks jolly—jollier indeed than the baby who invariably seems bowed down with a superabundance of clothing. In one picture, taken with Queen Mary, the year-old Elizabeth even seems to have acquired her first string of pearls; Granny, as usual, is wearing several.

When Margaret was born Mrs Knight's attentions were diverted and Elizabeth was taken over by the under-nurse, Margaret MacDonald. Throughout childhood 'Bobo' MacDonald, a somewhat blunt Scotswoman of working-class background, shared a bedroom with the Princess, then graduated in adult life to the position of 'dresser'. According to the Queen's biographer Robert Lacey, Bobo became one of her closest friends and confidantes and 'a unique sounding board, the closest contact Queen Elizabeth can have with the world she looks out at through limousine windows or the television screen.'

Whether Bobo has had any influence over anything except the Queen's clothes will always remain a matter of conjecture. But like all the people the Queen trusts, Bobo has been wonderfully discreet. It was the governess who let the side down. Alas poor Crawfie! Marion Crawford, another Scot, was hired as governess in 1932 and seems to have been exemplary in all that she did. Admonished by George v to teach the girls a 'decent hand' and by Queen Mary to pay more attention to history, geography and bible reading, she also managed to mix in swimming at the now defunct Bath Club and had the inspired idea of getting one or other of the royal paintings up from the vaults for a week's study. A Canaletto here, a Rubens there. She had a subscription to the goody-goody *Children's Newspaper* and took her charges to the zoo where they were photographed with the penguins. Bobo went too, looking dowdier and more sensible than

Crawfie who was really rather dashing with a very snappy line in hats.

After seventeen years Crawfie left to get married. Elizabeth Longford, another biographer royal, tells us that Crawfie scanned the honours' lists for a few years, looking in vain for the DCVO to which she felt entitled. Women have been made dames for less but Crawfie didn't make it. Lady Longford implies that this slight led the ex-governess to try her hand at authorship. *The Little Princesses* was followed by a column in *Woman's Own*. It was pretty harmless stuff—gushing, sycophantic—but 'The Royal Family feel she broke faith, irretrievably damaging the old system of trust.'

The contrast is intriguing: Bobo—commonsensical, unintellectual, loyal, good; Crawfie—imaginative, ambitious, academically inclined, disloyal, bad. When it came to bringing up her own children, Elizabeth sent them to boarding schools where that sort of influence was dissipated. Outside family it is difficult to think of any one person in the early lives of Charles, Anne, Andrew or Edward who made quite the impression that Bobo and Crawfie did on the present queen.

But the person who most changed her life was her uncle David. Until she was ten she was not, whatever Grandpapa England might hope, a woman born to be queen. However in 1936 the old king died; her uncle abandoned the crown for Mrs Simpson; her father became king of England and she the heir presumptive. The little family moved out of their agreeable private home in Piccadilly and across the park to the barn-like offices of Buckingham Palace. There was no way now that Princess Elizabeth could fulfil her once expressed ambition to be 'a lady living in the country with lots of horses and dogs.'

None of them wanted the job. George VI burst into tears when telling his mother what had happened; Crawfie said that the new queen, sitting up in bed with the 'flu, told her 'we must take what is coming and make the best of it'; Princess Elizabeth prayed for a baby brother who could one day become the monarch instead of her.

A year or two later Queen Mary remarked in a withering letter to her eldest son that 'All my life I have put my Country before everything else, and I simply cannot change now.' All her life Princess Elizabeth had been taught by her parents and grandparents—especially her grandparents—that royalty had duties and that those duties took precedence, even over the nursery card games like Old Maid and Happy Families, playing with the corgis or riding (though riding was part of her duty and she had had her own pony since 1929 when she was only three).

What was so especially galling was that the eldest brother was so apparently glamorous and dashing. That the Duke of Windsor was also a fairly hopeless case of arrested development only really became apparent later on. He had seemed cut out for kingship whereas the wretched Duke of York was a plodder like his father. He had a stammer which afflicted him in public speaking and he was quite lacking in what later came to be known as 'charisma'.

But the British came to cherish George VI for his ordinariness, just as they had enjoyed that quality in his father. Realizing this and mindful perhaps of the instability and lack of moral fibre which sometimes seems to accompany the more raffish qualities of royals such as Edward VIII or the short-lived and highly unsatisfactory Duke of Clarence, George VI and his elder daughter seem to have gone out of their way to cultivate ordinariness. In 1940 when she was fourteen, Elizabeth and her sister broadcast to the nation's children. Sitting there with her sensibly parted hair with its bobs at either side, with her sensible jumper under a sensible tweed jacket, staring very seriously at her script, the heir to the throne looks duller than she could possibly have been—perhaps she was working at it.

As she grew older lessons became more serious and more geared to her future role. The King would draw her attention to articles in *Punch* or *The Times*. Sir Henry Marten, vice-provost of Eton and the Marten of 'Warner and Marten', a partnership which was to History what Hillard and Botting was to the Classics, introduced her to Bagehot on the Constitution. And Crawfie hired French teachers. Mrs Montaudon-Smith was nicknamed 'Monty' with awful inevitability; and when another French tutor was taken on, a Belgian émigré called Antoinette de Bellaigue, the Princesses called her 'Toni'.

When war broke out the two princesses were on holiday in Scotland where the Strathmore castle at Glamis was a favourite retreat and where they could get to know cousins of a similar age. They stayed there for a while, then spent Christmas at Sandringham—having bought presents from Woolworths in Aberdeen. Afterwards they were sent to Windsor. There was some discussion about sending the princesses to Canada for the duration of the war but the Queen said the children wouldn't leave without her, she wouldn't leave without the King and the King was never leaving. Lessons at Windsor were sometimes interrupted by fire practice, a lesson in bomb disposal or a run across the east terrace to the slit trenches in the park.

At sixteen Elizabeth signed on at the labour exchange, as required by law. But not until just after her nineteenth birthday was she allowed to enlist in the ATS as a second subaltern based at the Camberley army depot. During the war she had, observes Robert Lacey, 'developed from a serious child into a serious girl with no discernible break in continuity'. She had also met the dashing Prince Philip. Indeed as early as 1941 Chips Channon had recorded with apparent certainty that Philip was to be 'Our Prince Consort'. But at the end of the war, when childhood was well and truly over, her father recorded of her and her sister 'Poor darlings, they have never had any fun yet.'

This does seem a slightly exaggerated verdict. Granted, despite her love of horses and racing, Princess Elizabeth had never attended a race meeting. Wartime security apparently made it impossible. But she and her sister starred in annual Windsor pantomimes and went to see Noel Coward's *In Which We Serve* being filmed. And at least she was able to give up maths when she found it boring and incomprehensible. Her mother, also the product of a home education, was not much fussed by an inability to do sums or pass School Cert. 'To spend as long as possible in the open air, to enjoy to the full the pleasures of the country, to be able to dance and draw and appreciate music, to acquire good manners and perfect deportment, and to cultivate all the distinctively feminine graces'—those were her mother's priorities.

The Queen Mother may not know a lot about nuclear physics or post-structuralist literary criticism, but as a training for monarchy her priorities are not far wrong. When your nearest approximation to 'normality' is belonging to a guide and brownie unit with its HQ in a hut in the gardens of Buckingham Palace, you have to accept that you are a little out of the ordinary.

The nearest Elizabeth has ever got to 'normal' or 'conventional' was the few years after her marriage. Her husband was a dashing young naval officer following a career and she was, almost, just another naval wife. This 'ordinary' couple's first son was born in 1948; they had a daughter just two years later. But normality was, of course, interrupted by accession and coronation.

The Queen's heir has had a more conventional upbringing and it seems probable that her grandson's will be more conventional yet. Whether that will enable them to do their job any more effectively remains to be seen. It is a very odd job and it seems quite probable that the odder the preparation the better.

With her mother in Windsor Royal Lodge in 1940, just before her 14th birthday.

Princess's progress: Elizabeth made her public bow through the stiff formality of her christening photograph (top left) taken on 26 May 1926. When she was three (below left) she was allowed to sit down during a public appearance on 12 June 1929. In March that year her grandfather was seriously ill and went to Bognor to convalesce. Elizabeth — a favourite of the old man's — was sent down to cheer him up (below, far left). At a wedding in October 1931 (centre right) her bearing gives a foretaste of what no one imagined was to come. She was often seen driving with her mother and grandmother (top right). The lovely, laughing girl with her corgi at Glamis in 1937 (below) seems to have no cares, but her public poses told a different story.

At a family wedding in 1936 (below) the Princess was still an interesting rather than significant public figure. But by the time her parents inspected the Royal Company of Archers on 5 July 1937 (right), her life had been radically altered. She may have been wearing the same outfit, but the Abdication on 10 December 1936 had transformed her status. After the Coronation on 12 May 1937, she took her place in the family group on the balcony at Buckingham Palace (above) as heir presumptive.

There's more than a touch of Millais in this romantic photograph (above) of Queen Elizabeth and her two daughters in 1937. By 1940 the princesses had been evacuated to Windsor (left), where their somewhat genteel private lessons continued. The King and Queen refused to send their children abroad during the war — earning the nation's gratitude.

On 6 May 1939, the King and Queen set off on an official tour of Canada. Seeing them off at the station — and looking a bit dubious about it all — were the two princesses (above). War was looming and some thought the tour too risky for the children.

While their parents were away, the girls were treated to a visit to London Zoo on 30 June 1939 (far left, below). Despite the four years separating them, the sisters were usually dressed alike (far left, above, Windsor 1940). This was quite usual at the time, but it made the older sister look younger. Rocking horses (left, August 1932) were soon to give way to the real thing.

During the war, the princesses amused themselves and charmed their guests by putting on a pantomime at Christmas. *Cinderella* in 1941 was followed by *Aladdin* (opposite page, top right) in 1943. The programme cover and cast list (opposite page, centre right) have quite a professional touch. In 1944 Princess Elizabeth was the heroine in *Old Mother Red Riding Boots* (opposite page, top left). Their wartime seclusion at Windsor was broken by a visit to Sandringham for the harvest in August 1943 (opposite page, bottom right). Joining the Girl Guides (opposite page, bottom left, in camp at Windsor in 1944) gave Princess Elizabeth a chance to meet other girls and learn some practical skill. But though she registered at the Labour Exchange in 1942 when she was 16, she wasn't allowed to join the ATS (Auxiliary Transport Service) until 1945, when she was nearly 19. Cecil Beaton photographed her in 1943 in uniform (above).

The first time Princess Elizabeth and Prince Philip were seen together was on 22 June 1939 at Dartmouth naval college (above) when she was 13 and he was 18. Philip, standing second right next to his uncle, Lord Mountbatten, was a cadet at Dartmouth. He had spent most of his life in Britain after his father — an officer in the Greek army and brother of the king — was banished following Greece's military disasters in Turkey. Eight years later the Princess celebrated her 21st birthday en route for South Africa (right). She had postponed her engagement at her father's request.

When Lord Mountbatten's daughter Patricia married Lord Brabourne on 26 October 1946, the two princesses were bridesmaids and Philip was an usher. His solicitous charge of the Princess (above) fuelled rumours of romance. The King was far from enthusiastic; Prince Philip had to become British (though later authorities have argued that he was all along), and the Princess had to go away on tour. Finally the engagement was announced and the official photograph taken at Buckingham Palace on 10 July 1947 (far left). The wedding (left), on 20 November 1947, cheered up a still impoverished postwar Britain.

When King George VI waved his daughter goodbye on her tour of Africa on 31 January 1952 (above left), it was the last time he saw her. He died on 6 February. She returned to Britain the next day, and was met at the airport as Queen by Churchill, Prime Minister, Attlee, Leader of the Opposition, Eden, Foreign Secretary, and the leaders of the Lords and Commons (above right). Shrouded in black, his widow and daughters met the King's body at King's Cross Station as it was brought from Sandringham for the lying in state (right). The people genuinely mourned the man who was not born to be king who had endured the war with them (below).

Coronation Day, 2 June 1953, dawned drizzly and chilly, but the crowd thought the sight of the Queen in the Golden Coach (bottom left) or on the Palace balcony (centre left) was worth getting wet for. As well as the invited guests, millions saw the scenes in the Abbey (top left) at home on the screen. It was television's first triumph. Street

parties were held all over Britain and local girls crowned queen, as in Swinbroke Road, Kensington (above). Less spontaneous tribute was paid by public figures, who launched into an extended drivel about the 'new Elizabethan age'. Scots were displeased by the title 'Elizabeth II', because Elizabeth I had had nothing to do with them.

John Grigg
A DELICATE BALANCE
The Queen and the constitution

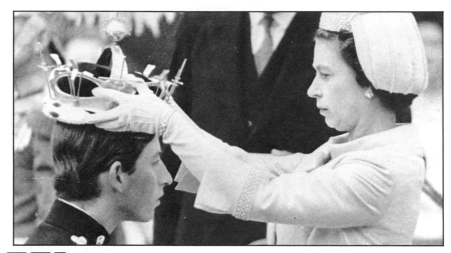

When Elizabeth II came to the throne in 1952 she was sovereign of only six countries—the United Kingdom, Canada, Australia, New Zealand, Ceylon and South Africa. She was also head of a Commonwealth that consisted of these six countries plus the republics of India and Pakistan. Today, the Commonwealth has a membership of forty-nine, and the Queen's role as its head has developed very significantly. Twenty-three Commonwealth countries are monarchies, and of these eighteen owe allegiance to her. (The remaining five monarchies—Malaysia, Brunei, Lesotho, Swaziland and Tonga—have their own indigenous monarchs.) Externally, therefore, the constitutional status of the British sovereign has changed almost out of recognition during the Queen's reign.

The change results, of course, from the dissolution of the British Empire, which was still a very substantial entity when the reign began. True, the Indian subcontinent was no longer under British rule, but in other parts of the world very large and/or populous territories still were. Although the India Office had ceased to exist, the Colonial Office remained an important and powerful ministry. There was still no ex-British independent state in black Africa, in the Caribbean or in South-East Asia, and in Europe Malta and Cyprus were still British colonies.

Now the British Empire survives only as a few outposts, which are either too small to be independent or for some other reason prefer to remain dependent upon Britain. The Colonial Office has followed the

At her Coronation in 1953 (right), as in her investiture of her eldest son as Prince of Wales in 1969 (left), the Queen embodies the British monarchy.

India Office into limbo, and the Dominions Office has been merged into the Foreign Office. There is still the Order of the British Empire, awarded in the main to what Falstaff calls 'inland petty spirits', but the great political organism from which it takes its name now belongs to history and the makers of television documentaries. The Imperial sun has set, and with it Britain's claim to be a superpower.

But—and this is the rather curious paradox—as the power of the British nation has declined, the prestige of its monarchy has increased. A constitutional evolution, not to say revolution, has taken place, transforming the British monarchy into a symbol of unity that people of almost every race and in every continent freely acknowledge. As head of the Commonwealth the Queen has no prerogatives, but the office is gradually acquiring the sort of acceptance, at both the official and popular levels, that inevitably gives its holder influence. That influence would soon disappear, however, if it were felt to be exercised on behalf of Britain. The Queen has to show that her role as head of the Commonwealth is a new one, which she performs for its own sake, and not as a continuation by other means of her traditional role as sovereign of the United Kingdom.

In many ways Elizabeth II has shown her awareness of this necessity and clearly does not confuse it with her position as British head of state, where she is subject to the advice of British ministers. It has become her habit to be present when Commonwealth heads of government meetings are held, and she is there very definitely as head of the Commonwealth, not as head of any particular country. The Queen's presence in the wings when Commonwealth leaders meet has political as well as social value, because she is able to meet them individually and collectively, and to discuss problems with them in an atmosphere of perfect confidence. At the same time, merely by being there she lends dignity and glamour to the occasion.

During the New Delhi conference in 1983, she was filmed discussing Commonwealth affairs with the late Indira Gandhi, prime minister of the host country, and the conversation was used in the Queen's ensuing Christmas broadcast. This provoked a good deal of criticism in Britain, and it was suggested that the Queen's words on such occasions should not be her own but should be written, or at any rate approved, by her British ministers. The criticism was, surely, quite wrong, and the Queen entirely right to disregard it. When she speaks at Christmas she is speaking to the Commonwealth as a whole, in her capacity as its head and not merely as Britain's queen. On such occasions she need not—indeed, she must not—serve as a mouthpiece for British government policy. The only valid criticism of the New Delhi broadcast might have come from Indians, since Mrs Gandhi was a controversial party politician in her own country. If her appearance with the Queen had been thought to benefit her politically, then opposition politicians in India had some reason to complain. But since the broadcast did not, in fact, become an issue in India, it was absurd for constitutional objections to be raised against it in Britain or anywhere else.

On the whole, Elizabeth II has shown an excellent understanding of her constitutional role as head of the Commonwealth, and has acted in such a way as to give it more meaning. But there are still a few blind spots. The composition of the Royal Household is very unbalanced, granted what the Queen is supposed to represent. While even the College of Cardinals has evolved from being overwhelmingly Italian to being overwhelmingly non-Italian, as befits the requirements of a universal church, the Queen's official entourage has remained almost exclusively British (and largely upper-class British). In particular, there are still no black or brown faces in the higher reaches of the Royal Household, which is inappropriate even in relation to the United Kingdom, now ethnically mixed, and far more so in relation to the Commonwealth. Certainly, there would be practical difficulty in changing this, but change it must, surely, if the Queen's establishment is to reflect her world-wide role.

It would make sense if there were two households and, more especially, two secretariats: one for the Commonwealth and one for Britain. But strict logic is seldom a good guide in such matters, and a sensible compromise might be that the Queen should continue to have, as at present, a single private secretary for all purposes, but that he or she should have two deputies, one concentrating on Commonwealth, the other on British business. Moreover, it is very important that the private secretary should not seem to be too narrowly British in character: in other words, the appointment should quite often be made from a country outside the United Kingdom.

One aspect of the Queen's constitutional position outside this country has proved troublesome through no fault of her own. This is the varying, at times contentious, role of her representatives in the Commonwealth countries of which she is sovereign. The worst case occurred in Australia in 1975, when the Governor-General, Sir John Kerr, dismissed Labour Prime Minister Gough Whitlam, appointed the opposition leader to succeed him, and then immediately granted a dissolution to the new prime minister. Although the election that followed confirmed the new government in office, the Queen's name was drawn into the argument and her popularity suffered.

Commonwealth ministers at Buckingham Palace in 1949; the Empire was officially laid to rest.

This was unfair, because the Queen had nothing whatever to do with Sir John Kerr's actions. A governor-general is a president in all but name, appointed on local advice, subject to the laws and constitutional conventions of the individual country, and in no political way responsible to the Queen. Although Kerr was, in fact, acting within his rights, what he did was of very questionable political wisdom, quite apart from its embarrassing implications for the monarchy. There seems to be no constitutional way of ensuring that such embarrassments will not occur again. The Queen has to rely upon her nominal representative to behave sensibly and with a proper regard for her interests, and hope public opinion in the country concerned eventually sees that a governor-general's actions are not hers, and might just as well be taken by a republican head of state.

At home, the sovereign is, so to speak, herself the governor-general, with political prerogatives that are more restricted than those of the governor-general of Australia but still not negligible. Since there are no fixed terms for elections here, and since our chief political executive is not elected as such, the Queen's right to dissolve Parliament and to appoint prime ministers remains significant. Of course, for the monarchy's sake it is vital that she should try to avoid any imputation of partisanship. So far as dissolving Parliament is concerned, this means that she should normally stick to the safe rule of acting on the advice of the prime minister of the day, whatever his or her party. And in the matter of appointing a prime minister, the equally safe rule is that the person to choose is the leader of the largest party in the House of Commons, who is likely to be able to command a majority there. Unfortunately neither of these rules can be regarded as foolproof. Elizabeth II has had eight prime ministers to date, and in most cases their appointment has been a straightforward affair. But there have been three awkward moments.

The first arose out of a hypothetical situation which occurred in the summer of 1953, when Churchill was paralysed by a stroke and seemed on the point of death. His 'heir apparent' Anthony Eden was also ill at the time, and the Queen was persuaded to agree that, in the event of Churchill's death, she would appoint a stopgap prime minister in the person of Lord Salisbury, on the understanding that he would resign and make way for Eden if and when the latter returned to health. It was lucky for the Queen that Churchill recovered and she was saved from having to give effect to this arrangement, which would have been a constitutional and political outrage in more ways than one. The best, if not the only, defence of her agreement to it is that she was very new to the job.

Four years later, when Eden resigned the prime ministership after Suez, there was no consensus in the Conservative Party over who should succeed him. The party still had no open and above-board procedure for deciding the leadership and the Queen seemed to be implicated in the arcane processes whereby Harold Macmillan emerged as the new party leader. The issue was decided behind the scenes, the Queen was informed, and the nation first knew who had won when she sent for Macmillan and appointed him prime minister. It appeared that the sovereign herself had played a part in choosing a new leader for the Conservative Party. In fact she had done nothing of the sort, and she would therefore have been fully justified in telling the incoming premier that his party must adopt a new method for choosing its leaders, so that she would never again be placed in such a false position. Unfortunately she failed to do so, with the result that she found herself in an even more invidious position when Macmillan himself resigned in 1963. In 1957, at the time of Eden's resignation, she was still very inexperienced, but she should not have allowed herself to be compromised by the Tories a second time.

The Queen has yet to face a situation in which the leader of the largest party in the House is unable to command a majority there. The nearest she came to it was after the first general election of 1974, which returned Labour as the largest party in the House but without an overall majority. For a short time the incumbent prime minister, Edward Heath, tried to form a majority through inter-party negotiation, as he was entitled to do. But when it became obvious that he could not succeed, he at once resigned and the Queen was then free to send for the Labour Party leader, Harold Wilson.

It is highly probable that before the end of her reign, perhaps after the next election, Elizabeth may have to wrestle with the problem of choosing a prime minister in a hung parliament; worse still, she may have to decide whether or not to grant a dissolution in such conditions. If, for instance, Labour were returned as the largest single party but were still a minority in the House, and if the other two main elements were unable to combine to form a sustainable majority, obviously it would be right for the Queen to send for the Labour leader. But would she be right to grant him an early dissolution if he made no attempt to negotiate for majority support, and if, after a few weeks or months, the other parties got together on an agreed programme? On the face of it she would be justified, both in the national interest and to avoid the appearance of favouring the Labour Party, in refusing to dissolve and inviting somebody else to try to form a government within the existing House. Only if and when it appeared that no majority government could be formed would it be obligatory, or even proper, for the Queen to plunge the country into another election. But much would, of course, depend upon how long the parliament had run and upon the state of public opinion.

The Queen's constitutional sense may be more severely tested in the years ahead than it has been to date. If three-party politics have come to stay, her constitutional role in Britain may become more important and more difficult than it has ever been.

As she matured, Princess Elizabeth was coached in her duties. She was introduced to the despatch boxes by her father (bottom, 11 April 1942) and acquired her own desk in the Palace (bottom, centre, 19 July 1946). The bestowing of honours is a pleasant task (bottom, centre right, knighting Francis Chichester on 7 July 1967). The distribution by the Monarch of Maundy Money is a hardy annual (below, in 1935, and right in 1984).

The relationship between the Queen and Parliament (left) is one of those niceties of the (unwritten) British constitution that can drive outside observers to despair and insiders to labyrinthine explanations. One fact is quite clear: the annual sessions of Parliament cannot begin until Her Majesty opens them, a splendid occasion enjoyed by all MPs — well, nearly all — and many of the public through television. Above right: the state opening in 1972. Nor is the British Parliament the only one she has opened: she is seen on the right in Canada in 1977.

Trooping the Colour, in all weathers, is one of the Queen's most important ceremonial duties (above, right and far right, top). The Yeomen of the Guard (far right, bottom), the Sovereign's bodyguard, is the world's oldest military corps. As well as having this ceremonial guard, the Queen is discreetly guarded at all times. Except, as became alarmingly clear in July 1982 when an intruder got into her bedroom, at home in the Palace.

The chivalric orders are an important medium of pageantry and patronage; the Knights of the Garter service takes place annually at Windsor (right, 1974) on St George's Day. It's the oldest order, founded in 1348. As head of state the Queen is head of the Church of England; at Windsor at Christmas 1984 she is neatly flanked by powers spiritual and temporal (above).

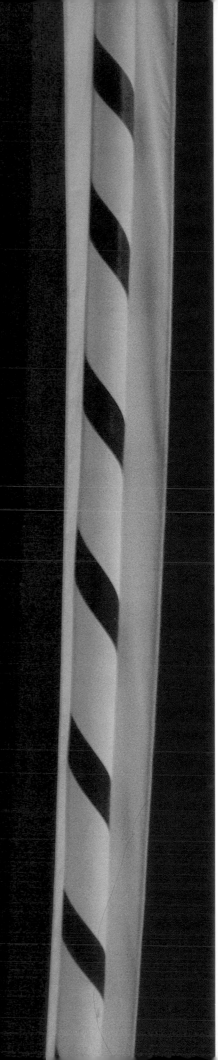

Acting as hostess to official guests from other countries is a task the Queen seems to enjoy, especially when she receives someone like Dr Hastings Banda of Malawi (left, at Windsor in April 1985) whom she has known for many years. She has received many rulers and leaders at Windsor, Balmoral and Buckingham Palace and has seen several thrones fall. The visit of Emperor Hirohito of Japan in October 1971 (above) was not a popular one; many still regarded him as a war criminal.

Alan Watkins
ALL THE QUEEN'S MEN
The Monarch and her ministers

When he was a cabinet minister, the late Richard Crossman said to the Queen's principal private secretary that Her Majesty would understandably feel more at ease with Conservatives and probably missed Alec Douglas-Home as prime minister. The secretary seemed genuinely puzzled. Oh no, he replied, not at all: to the Queen, all politicians looked very much the same. Still, it is no secret that she gets on better with some than with others. Of recent prime ministers, in fact, Labour figures have been more popular at the palace than Conservatives.

Harold Wilson was prouder of his friendly relationship with the Queen than of virtually anything else. He told her the date of the 1970 general election months in advance, before she set off on an official visit to New Zealand. She was one of the first to know about his resignation six years later. When Rhodesia declared independence in 1965, Wilson quite deliberately involved her on his and the then government's behalf. For instance, when the Rhodesian prime minister Ian Smith sent a message to the Queen saying that whatever happened his countrymen would never swerve in their loyalty, Her Majesty replied that she was confident that 'all her Rhodesian people will demonstrate their loyalty by continuing to act in a constitutional manner.' Arguably, it was perfectly correct for Wilson to advise her to send this reply and that both of them, Queen and prime minister alike, would have been failing in their duty if they had done anything else. Nevertheless, the Government's handling of the Rhodesian declaration of independence was a matter of controversy between the parties in Britain. It could also be argued—though less convincingly, perhaps—that the Queen was lending her authority to one side.

The immediate point is, however, that she and Harold Wilson got on well together. They spent hours talking to each other, her children's education being a favourite subject of conversation.

James Callaghan was equally devoted but more deferential. According to Richard Crossman, when the Cabinet was discussing a royal pay claim made by Prince Philip—this was before Callaghan became prime minister, when he was home secretary—he told his colleagues that he was 'a loyalist. I would not like to see the royal family hurt and I think Philip is a very fine fellow.' Crossman noted that he and his Labour colleagues Barbara Castle and Roy Jenkins were republicans. They did not like the position of the Royal Family. They did not like going to court or feel comfortable there. And they knew that the

The Queen had known her first Prime Minister Winston Churchill (right, above) for some years and he was sentimentally fond of her. But the relationship between the Sovereign and her most recent chief minister, Margaret Thatcher (right, below), is rumoured to be less cordial. No hint of this shows in public.

Queen was not comfortable with them. Whatever Jenkins's views may have been—and to describe them as 'republican' implies a zeal which he is not accustomed to display over most matters—Mrs Castle was certainly favourably impressed by the Queen. Though she refused to curtsy to her, a refusal which did not appear to cause any unpleasantness, she paid several tributes to Her Majesty's naturalness and wish to put ministers at their ease.

Crossman takes the view, and it is probably valid enough, that the less exalted socially, or intellectually (or both), a minister was, the more royalist he or she turned out to be. He recorded that Fred Peart was 'appalled' at the hostility displayed in the Cabinet towards the royal pay rise. Not only did he think it was politically unwise to give any anti-monarchical taint to their actions as a Labour government, he also, according to Crossman, 'adored' being lord president of the council and got on with the Queen just as Lord George-Brown and James Callaghan did. Indeed the former, according to Barbara Castle's account, used to be affectionately familiar with Her Majesty, calling her 'my dear'. Elizabeth did not seem to mind this—or, if she did, she did not show it.

The Queen did not get on especially well with Harold Macmillan, now Lord Stockton, when he was prime minister. She was particularly upset about the Profumo case in 1963. Sir Alec Douglas-Home was more to her liking. But Edward Heath she found stiff and unbending, as perhaps he found her. And she does not really hit it off with Margaret Thatcher either.

Not that it is easy to get on familiar terms with the Monarch. After a visit to Balmoral, Lord Elwyn-Jones, then attorney-general, wanted to write to the Queen because he had enjoyed himself so much there. He consulted Sir Neville Leigh, the Clerk to the Privy Council, about the correct way to go about this. 'Well, of course, she doesn't like you to write just to the Private Secretary and ask him to tell her how much you enjoyed it,' Sir Neville said. 'If you write she likes you to write personally to her.'

'That's just what I want to do. But how do I address her?'

'It's so complicated I'll have to write it down.'

'Letter to the Queen,' Sir Neville wrote. 'This should begin: "Madam, with my humble duty", continue with what you wish to say, and end: "I am, Madam, your Majesty's most humble and obedient subject". The envelope should be addressed to the Queen at Buckingham Palace and bear your initials at the bottom right-hand corner.'

'I can't write a decent bread-and-butter letter enclosed in those appalling formalities. Do I really have to?'

'Of course,' Sir Neville insisted. 'You couldn't write anything different from that. That's what she has to get from anybody who writes to her, however personally, including one of her ministers.'

In between Winston Churchill and Margaret Thatcher there have been six other prime ministers: two Labour politicians – Harold Wilson (centre right) and James Callaghan (bottom right) – and four Tories – Anthony Eden (top left), Harold Macmillan (top right), Alec Douglas-Home (centre left) and Edward Heath (bottom right). It is said that on the whole Labour figures have been more popular at the palace than Conservative ones.

The Queen's formal dealings with cabinet ministers fall roughly into these categories: meetings of the Privy Council; the swearing-in of ministers to the Privy Council; transfers of seals of office; meetings with the Lord President of the Council; and discussions with the Prime Minister, once every week or so, when Parliament is sitting and both are in Britain.

Meetings of the Privy Council move around, depending on whether the Queen is in London, Sandringham, Balmoral or Windsor. The quorum is four. First, the Lord President goes in to see the Queen on his own with the papers for the meeting. They chat for a minute or two. Then the others enter and line up beside him. He reads aloud the titles of the orders in council—there may be as many as sixty—pausing after every half-dozen or so for her to say 'Agreed'. When the Lord President has finished, usually in three or four minutes, he says: 'So the business of the council is concluded.' Then there is polite talk with lunch, tea or drinks, as the time of day indicates.

There are times when the Queen asks the Prime Minister for advice. In 1967, for example, she inquired about the remarriage of Lord Harewood. She had to take this course because, at the time, he was eighteenth in succession to the throne and accordingly came under the Royal Marriages Act 1772. If she had not asked for advice the Cabinet would presumably have been entitled to proffer it anyway, whether yea or nay, off its own bat. On this occasion, everything was all right, and the Cabinet's permission was given to the Queen at a meeting of the Privy Council.

There are other times when the Queen tries to intervene in politics. It is considered disloyal, or even downright treasonable, to point this out, but it is true. One of the best recent illustrations concerned the late Emrys Hughes's Abolition of Titles bill. Hughes was a popular but egotistical parliamentary joker, whose origins lay in the old Independent Labour Party. His private member's bill had even less chance than most of ever becoming law. In any case, it was directed not so much at the Queen and her titles, which would have been left unaffected by it, as at the House of Lords. The Queen, however, took alarm. Certainly her private secretary, Sir Michael Adeane, did. He asked Harold Wilson—this was during his premiership in 1967—to stop the bill. Richard Crossman, as lord president, and Roy Jenkins, home secretary, both advised Her Majesty personally, in writing, that blocking Hughes's bill would be misunderstood. Sir Michael then went back to the Prime Minister and convinced him that the measure should indeed be prevented from being debated. Wilson put this to the Cabinet, but was then persuaded by Crossman and Jenkins that the debate should be held. This duly happened, nothing came of it, and the Queen breathed again.

One of the most serious Palace-cum-political crises since 1945 occurred over the American invasion of Grenada, an independent

Commonwealth country of which the Queen is head of state. Though Margaret Thatcher and Elizabeth II found themselves on the same side in this instance—they both deplored the United States intervention and, it is fair to say, for roughly the same reason, that of hurt pride—the Queen's complaint was that she was not kept fully enough informed of what was going on. However, the Government did not seem to be any too well informed itself on this occasion.

All new cabinet ministers kiss hands. This is not because they are being made ministers but because they are being sworn into the Privy Council. All privy councillors are allowed to preface their names 'Rt Hon.'—'PC' after the name is a solecism—and membership is not limited to the cabinet ranks: some have been given the title as a sort of political consolation prize (Roy Hattersley successfully besought Harold Wilson to make him a privy councillor) or because they are party leaders, such as Neil Kinnock and David Steel. The drill is as follows . . .

There is a rehearsal in the privy council office, which lasts about an hour. A Buckingham Palace official teaches the new councillors how to stand up, how to kneel on one knee on a cushion, how to raise the right hand with the bible in it, how to advance three paces towards the Queen, how to take her hand and go through the motions of kissing it, and how to move backwards ten paces without falling over the stools—which have been carefully arranged so that they will fall over them. Then the privy councillors are driven to the palace in their official cars and stand about in an ante-room until they are summoned into a large drawing room. At the end is the Queen, standing, with her hand on the table. It takes something over half an hour to get through a dozen or so privy councillors.

Once there was a great shambles involving a Conservative cabinet of the 1950s. The ministers got themselves into the wrong positions and started to crawl about, making roughly for the Queen. She looked furious. Afterwards her private secretary apologized, saying she must have been very angry—she had certainly looked it. Not at all, she replied: she had been forced to put on that face to stop herself laughing.

Political opponents have accused Mrs Thatcher of delusions of regality; Her Majesty's opinion is unknown.

Sue Arnold

FAMILY MATTERS

Majesty and motherhood

With new additions to the Royal Family arriving at regular intervals like tax demands—in the last ten years there have been four royal grandchildren and four royal first cousins, all receiving the usual adulatory attention of the media along with their radiant young mothers—it is easy to forget that the Queen too is a mother. No longer young, less radiant than ripened, but none the less a mother of four, the youngest two still living at home.

The public image of the British Family Windsor is as regular as apple pie. There they stand at all those public family gatherings, christenings, memorial services, Royal Ascot, neatly lined up like cardboard cut-outs on the back of a cornflakes packet, cheese-ing dutifully out at the cameras: as wholesome as the Waltons, as harmonious as the Oxo family, as happy as Bisto kids. We know what the Queen thinks about family life because she has aired her views in public. Speaking at a silver jubilee luncheon given by the Lord Mayor of London at the Guildhall she said, 'When the Bishop was asked what he thought about sin he replied with simple conviction, "I'm against it." If I am asked today what I think about family life after twenty-five years of marriage I can answer with equal simplicity and conviction, "I am for it." '

We know something about life behind the palace gates thanks to television documentaries and a plethora of women's magazine exposés. We know they have supper on trays in front of the television. We know they like giving funny presents—corgi-shaped soap is a favourite stocking filler for Mum. Years ago, as a student working in Harrods, I saw Prince Charles, doing his Christmas shopping armed with a long list. I sold him a purple candle in the shape of some Eastern deity which he said was just what his mother would like.

But take a closer look at the family photograph. Beneath the bland formality it is possible to detect chinks in the armour of Mrs Majesty the Monarch and her Happy Family. Look for instance at Miss Majesty the Monarch's daughter. Have you noticed how she invariably stands next to her father? This is no accident. Of all his children Philip is closest to his daughter, possibly because she's the most like his side of the family in looks and character. Anne has the tall, slim, Mountbatten build, the strong features, long nose and pendulous lower lip. She has her father's temperament too, his stubborn streak, impatience, wilfulness, determination and boisterous Hooray Henry

Princess Elizabeth's first son, Charles Philip Arthur George, was born on 14 November 1948. Cecil Beaton's study of mother and baby (right) could be a generation earlier, so little had styles for royal babies changed.

Anne, born 15 August 1950 and christened Anne Elizabeth Alice Louise, has a special kinship with her father. Here they tend the Balmoral barbecue in October 1972.

attitude to life. This and her somewhat motherless upbringing draw her close to Philip and away from her mother—with whom she has little in common apart from an obsession with horses. But the 'intruder-in-the-palace' incident, when Michael Fagan broke into the Queen's bedroom and sat on her bed, changed the somewhat stiff mother/daughter relationship, according to friends. When the furore was over the Queen retreated, shattered, to Balmoral. She was closer then to a complete breakdown than at any time in her life. Anne left Gatcombe Park, her Gloucestershire home, and flew to Balmoral. She and her mother went for long walks together, talking as they had never talked to each other before. It seems that it took Fagan to put the Queen's relationship with her only daughter on a new footing.

Let us turn now to Master Majesty the Monarch's eldest son. He prefers to stand a little apart from the group, never next to his father and usually one or two siblings removed from his mother's side. Poor Charles. So much was expected, demanded of him. All he wanted as a child was an ordinary family. Instead he got a mother who abandoned him before he was four to become ruler of a quarter of the world's population and a father who wanted him to be Action Man. That toughening up at Gordonstoun—leaping from aeroplanes, deep-sea diving—it was all done to gratify his parent's image of what a prince of Wales should be. Now at last he has got what he wanted: his own home, a loving wife (who also had a miserable childhood), two kids. But when he says he just wants to stay home and play with them everyone thinks he's gone loopy. If Granny Majesty the Monarch's Mother were in the portrait, Charles would be standing next to her—he is closer to his grandmother than anyone else in the family, with Aunt Margaret a close second.

But remember that Mrs Majesty the Monarch has *four* children. In our royal portrait Master Andrew stands wedged so close to his mother they might be rush-hour commuters on the Victoria Line, with Master Edward hugging her on the other side. These two have often been called the Queen's second family: her *normal* family. When they were born a decade after the first batch, Elizabeth was eager to experience the pleasures and rewards of real family life without the awful pressures that had accompanied her introduction to motherhood. The familiarity of the Queen's relationship with her second son is something Charles hardly knew. Andrew can tickle his mother and poke her in the ribs till she begs him to stop. When Edward comes

Charles and his grandmother have always been close; Lisa Sheridan photographed them at Windsor in 1954, with a dog sadly lacking in pedigree.

70

home for college vacation his mother makes scrambled eggs and they sit in her private drawing room and chat about Cambridge. But between the Queen and Charles there has seldom been such horseplay or warmth. They visit each other by invitation only. Since his marriage, the Queen has been twice to Highgrove for afternoon tea.

How has this curiously divided family situation developed? Elizabeth's premature accession to the throne on the sudden death of George VI is the most obvious reason for the distancing of the two elder children. A few months after the coronation, at a time when Charles was only five and Anne three, Queen Elizabeth and the Duke of Edinburgh left for a gruelling six-month tour of the Commonwealth, leaving their children in the care of nannies. It is no secret that Mabel Anderson, the chief nurse, favoured Anne, making a great pet of the pretty golden-haired toddler, while Charles—reticent and introvert by nature and more affected by the separation from his parents—suffered in silent misery. He turned to Granny for comfort and she gave it willingly. When the Queen and Duke returned from that first long Commonwealth tour, they were met at the station by the Queen Mother and the two children. Charles in short pants and clean white socks was led forward by his grandmother to 'say hello to Mummy'. He hesitated, hung his head and then shyly took her outstretched hand and shook it.

All might not have been lost at this early stage had the Queen not been so dominated by her husband. It is no exaggeration to say that when she married him, Elizabeth was head over heels in love with Philip. This was no arranged marriage but for her part a genuine romance. She idolized her tall, handsome, macho sailor husband who drank with the boys, played polo with Uncle Dickie Mountbatten and went off and had a game of squash while she gave birth to their first child. The infatuation has not diminished after nearly forty years of marriage. Even darling Andrew plays second fiddle to his father in the Queen's affections. So the Duke's views on child-rearing automatically became hers. Children should be seen and not heard. Boys should be tough, young men should be allowed to sow their wild oats. Philip was never that fond of small children—or 'brats' as he was inclined to call them.

The Queen and Duke of Edinburgh broke with royal tradition by sending their children away to boarding school: Charles to his father's Alma Mater, Gordonstoun; Anne to Benenden, deep in stockbroker Kent. The boisterous, thick-skinned princess coped well with the extrovert life of public school. She had a clique of friends whom she would invite to join her for exeats when her parents drove down for Sunday lunch at the George Hotel in nearby Cranbrook. The royal couple would be treated to the usual schoolgirl horror stories of institutional food—rats' bones (corned beef), frogspawn (sago), disaster on the Alps (semolina with strawberry jam).

At five and a half Charles is already his familiar self as he strides along the quay in Malta with his Uncle Dickie (Lord Mountbatten).

Meanwhile 600 miles north, Charles was hating Gordonstoun. Before his arrival the other pupils had been instructed to treat the new boy normally. The briefing had the opposite effect. So anxious were they not to be seen to be sucking up to their future king that the boys shunned him. Charles had few friends. He didn't shine academically nor was he much good at sport—to the disappointment of his father. Although he plays polo, it is without Philip's flair. That's the story of Charles's life. He has always been overshadowed by his father. Where the Duke is quick-witted, charming, relaxed, Charles takes time to grasp facts and is still shy. The one thing he does do better than his father is ski, a sport Philip regards as wet.

Because of Gordonstoun's remoteness, Charles rarely saw his parents during term. When the family holiday at Balmoral ended, everyone else returned to London for the routine of weekdays at Buckingham Palace and Windsor at weekends. Sometimes the Queen Mother stayed on in Scotland visiting friends and if she were near, she would call in at Gordonstoun, bringing Charles his favourite Mars bars or Fry's peppermint creams. He counted on these visits. He once threw his arms round her, burst into tears and begged her to persuade his father to take him away from school because he was so miserable. She was sympathetic but firm. She would not interfere. A stiff upper lip was the rule for Charles. His mother impressed on him the importance of self-control and usually he succeeded. On the few occasions he did crack it was never in front of his parents; his mother would have been embarrassed, his father scornful. Instead, he sought other confidantes: his grandmother, his aunt and especially his godmother Aunt Peg (Princess Margaret of Hesse—she was the person he telephoned first, in tears, when he learnt of Uncle Dickie's murder by the IRA).

Andrew on the other hand *is* Action Man; but then his upbringing was entirely different. The story has it that Andrew was the result of a reconciliation between the Queen and Prince Philip, who for some time had been going through a sticky patch in their marriage. Elizabeth's reaction to the birth of her third child was as rapturous as if he had been the first—and in a way he was. Andrew's self-confidence has all the hallmarks of the spoiled child. His parents are justifiably proud of his Falklands service. His mother secretly admires the Randy Andy image. Of course sometimes he goes too far. Like the time he sprayed press photographers with white paint. It was Philip who gave him a dressing-down for that; his mother felt he had been punished enough by the publicity and the shame. Ten years earlier, when Anne was receiving a bad press for her 'naff off' remarks, it was Mum who scolded, Dad who thought it all a big joke. Philip has never had much regard for the press either.

While no one could describe the Queen as a cosy mother—she belongs to a generation that didn't change nappies or stick around at bathtime, unlike Anne and Charles who don't mind the messy side of parenthood—she obviously enjoys family life. Summer holidays in Balmoral are sacred. When the two younger boys were little she would pack them into the back of the car, drive them to the village sweet shop and buy bulls' eyes. The sequence most remembered in Richard Cawston's television documentary, 'Royal Family', made for the BBC in 1969, is the riverside barbecue. It's all pretty humdrum. Anne turns the sausages, Philip is having problems with the fire. The Queen in tweed jacket and pearls fixes the salad while Charles mixes French dressing with the concentration of a neuro-surgeon performing a lobotomy. 'What's it like?' he asks his mother nervously. 'Oily,' she snaps and goes back to the tomatoes. It may just be that he's camera shy but the Duke looks as if he'd rather be somewhere else.

During their time at Balmoral the family take a holiday within a holiday, spending time in a remote fishing lodge without aides, attendants or servants. The Queen cooks (Bird's custard features a lot), the Duke dries the dishes, daughter-in-law Diana peels potatoes. This is exactly the kind of mother image the Queen relishes.

There is a family ritual of Sunday afternoon tea at Windsor Castle with everyone present including her favourite grandchild Peter Phillips. The corgis snooze by the fire and at four o'clock the tea trolley is wheeled in. The Queen presides at the head of a table loaded with sandwiches, hot buttered crumpets, chocolate cake. 'Now then,' she says lifting the huge silver teapot, 'who's ready for tea?' As a surprise for his wife Prince Philip once invented a self-pouring teapot. It was a sort of tilting stand on which the teapot rested, which meant she no longer had to heave such a weight. The Queen refused to have it on the table and never ever used it. 'I like playing mother,' she said.

Patrick Lichfield's photograph of the royal parents with senior offspring Anne and Charles and juniors Andrew and Edward at Balmoral in 1972.

Since his mother was heir to the throne, Prince Charles was the most publicized baby of his day, from his christening onwards. He took his bow in the family gown (right, with his mother, grandmother Queen Elizabeth, and great-grandmother Queen Mary and, below, with his mother) on 15 December 1948. The three royal ladies wore the same outfits for Princess Anne's christening on 21 October 1950 — and so, of course, did the baby. At the Coronation (opposite page, top left) his grandmother and Aunt Margaret helped explain things. Balmoral was the place where Charles could indulge in ordinary childhood activities (opposite page, below, in 1952), and a holiday in Malta with Lord and Lady Mountbatten in 1954 was a great treat (this page, bottom right). In 1956 the Queen was snapped at the wheel of her Daimler in Windsor, taking the children for a drive (opposite page, top right).

Anne always looked less convincing in frilly dresses (opposite page, bottom left, in 1957 on her seventh birthday, a photograph taken by Tony Armstrong- Jones) than in tomboy rig such as riding or sailing gear. She seemed demure enough when waiting for her mother to come back from Canada on 22 October 1957 (below), but other pictures revealed her resolute nature. Horses were always her great passion (opposite page, top, with William, the pony she and Charles both learned to ride on, in 1959). The Queen's pride in her daughter's equestrian skill shines through the photograph taken in 1971 (opposite page, bottom right) when she congratulated her on her wins at the annual Burghley horse trials in Lincolnshire.

The Queen's children are an active bunch and quite ready to court danger on land, sea or in the air: Charles is equally at home windsurfing (top left) or at the controls of a Hawk (top right). Edward pitches in on the rugby field (above left), while Andrew (above right) is a battle-hardened helicopter pilot. Polo is Charles's particular joy (right and far right, bottom). Anne sticks to horses (and sometimes comes unstuck) and is a first-class rider (far right, top).

Andrew, first of the Queen's 'second family', was born on 19 February 1960, nearly ten years later than his sister (above left, 27 March 1960). He was only rarely seen in public. Then the Falklands War made him a national hero (left, meeting his mother on his return from action, and right, at the Falklands memorial service in June 1983). The Press made him another kind of hero as 'Randy Andy', a nickname he says he acquired at school.

The Queen's two younger boys — Edward was born on 10 March 1964 — spent their childhood out of the public glare. So much so that there were occasional whispers that there was something wrong with them. That this was clearly nonsense is shown in the photograph (above) of Charles driving the

five-year-old Edward in a
go-kart at Windsor in
April 1969. As shown by
his fairytale *The Old Man
of Lochnagar* (published in
1980 but written in the

sixties), Charles was much
involved with his little
brothers. The boys were
usually seen with their
mother on informal
occasions: the

two-year-old Andrew
travelling with the Queen
(top left), Edward at
Badminton in 1976 (centre
left), and both of them
together at Windsor (left).

Like many a girl who was dubbed a tomboy for rejecting dolls and daintiness, Anne had a special bond with her father (top left, on the polo field). His pride in her is clear to see as he leads her up the aisle in Westminster Abbey on her wedding day 14 November 1973 (above). Anne chose for her husband the solidly middle-class Mark Phillips, a captain serving with the Queen's Dragoon Guards who shares her interest in horses (top right). The couple met while competing in the Mexico Olympics in 1968 and rumours of their attachment spread after the Munich Olympics in 1972.

The announcement of Charles's engagement on 27 March 1981 to Lady Diana Spencer ended years of frenzied speculation. Lady Diana was young, beautiful and, as commentators pointed out at length, of impeccable pedigree (though there was the unfortunate fact of her parents' divorce). The wedding in St Paul's on 29 July 1981 (left) was the grandest royal occasion since the Coronation. The bride's dress by the Emanuels was not universally admired, but the bride herself was. Princess Diana has subsequently become the most potent icon of British womanhood.

First of the Queen's grandchildren, born in 1977, was Peter Phillips (top left, at Badminton in 1983). His sister, Zara (left, at Windsor in 1984), arrived in 1981. They are often to be seen with their grandmother, but otherwise they will not be 'involved' in the royal system. No such fortune attends Charles's elder son, William, born 1982 (top right), nor the second, Henry (above, at his christening on 21 December 1984).

Whether bleakly enduring the rain at Badminton (far left, with Lord Snowdon) or playfully enjoying the fresh air in the Highlands (above), the Queen is often at her most natural with her mother and sister. Norman Parkinson's photograph of the three of them on the Queen Mother's 80th birthday on 4 August 1980 (left) emphasizes their closeness. When the Queen kissed her sister goodnight after a gala at Covent Garden in 1984 (left, below), their affection was clearly unstudied.

No account of the Queen's family loyalties would be complete without her dogs. From childhood she has been surrounded by them — and they have followed her (left: a corgi pup escaped from six-year-old Prince Andrew and made for the Queen as she inspected a guard of honour at Balmoral in August 1966. An equerry captured it just in time). Dogs crowd around her when she's off duty (above), race before her by the sea in Norfolk (above, centre, July 1984), and, together with the wheel of the aircraft steps, generally inhibit her mobility (far left, Heathrow, 1984).

Donald Trelford
WHAT THE PAPERS SAY
———————— The Palace and the press ————————

King George VI is said to have kept a scrapbook which he called 'Things my daughters never did'. It's a story Michael Shea, the Queen's press secretary, is unable to confirm, but he comments: 'I only know that when, from time to time, I have attempted to keep a list or catalogue of the fictional stories written about the Royal Family, I ended up with writer's cramp after the first day.'

France Dimanche, the Paris newspaper with an insatiable curiosity about the British Royal Family, once calculated that it had carried 63 reports of the Queen's proposed abdication, 73 reports of her divorce, 115 reports of rows with the Earl of Snowdon, 17 reports of rudeness to Princess Grace of Monaco, and 92 reports of her being pregnant. The paper added proudly that two of these last reports had turned out to be true. That catalogue covered only a part of the Queen's reign, so the total volume of lies and nonsense must now be many times greater, with Prince Charles, Princess Diana and Prince Andrew begetting further generations of titillating untruths.

The British Embassy in Paris used to send copies of *France Dimanche* to Buckingham Palace for Her Majesty's private amusement. Such an arrangement can hardly be needed now, for the invention of royal fairy tales has become a flourishing growth industry within our native press. And yet, for all this 'clap-trap', as Michael Shea calls it—and frequent headlines like 'Queen Upset by Fleet Street' or 'Palace in new press row' that might suggest otherwise—'there is no war between the Palace and the press'. And that's official. As Mr Shea told the Guild of British Newspaper Editors, 'Why should there be a war when 100 per cent of the coverage in the regional press and 99 per cent—well, let's say 98 per cent—in the national press, is positive and enormously well disposed towards the Queen and her family? We all know that these Royal stories sell newspapers.'

It is refreshing to hear that—and of course it is true. For all the 'clap-trap' written about the private lives of the Royal Family, the intrusions and the annoyance thus provoked, and the occasional disgruntled murmurs about the cost of the Civil List, the British press remains as loyal, even sycophantic, towards the institution of monarchy as it was at the time of the Queen's coronation more than thirty years ago. There is no newspaper today—and no political party represented in Parliament—which supports republicanism even as a long-term objective. The editor of one of our most radical weeklies

Photographers almost hemming her in and practically blocking her path have become a familiar hazard (here, Portugal 1985). The Queen is said to admire their skill at scurrying backwards.

complains wryly that not only are people uninterested in reading attacks on the monarchy, but few journalists feel impelled to write them any more.

It is hard, looking back, to understand the fierce passions aroused in 1957 by the comments on the monarchy made by John Grigg, then Lord Altrincham, in the *National and English Review*. He complained the royal style was out of date, that the court was too 'tweedy', and that the speeches prepared for the Queen were too stuffy: 'The personality conveyed by the utterances which are put into her mouth is that of a priggish schoolgirl, captain of the hockey team, a prefect and a recent candidate for confirmation.' The press rushed to the young queen's defence, echoing with relish the response of the Earl of Strathmore ('Young Altrincham is a bounder—he should be shot!') and the Duke of Argyll ('I would like to see the man hanged, drawn and quartered!'). Not that the indignation was confined to aristocrats: eight 'Teddy boys' sent Grigg a threatening letter, the town of Altrincham disowned its eponymous lord, and villagers daubed 'God Save the Queen' in letters three-foot high on the wall of his mother's house.

Malcolm Muggeridge fared as badly when he dared to criticize 'the royal soap opera' as a 'sort of substitute or ersatz religion'. He was banned by the BBC, sacked as a columnist by the *Sunday Dispatch* and resigned from the Garrick Club. It was open season on the royals that year, for John Osborne, flushed with the success of *Look Back in Anger*, weighed in with a diatribe of his own, describing the monarchy as 'the last circus of a civilization that has lost faith in itself and sold itself for a splendid triviality. My objection to the Royal symbol is that it is dead; it is a gold filling in a mouth full of decay.' Paradoxically, the effect of all these attacks was to revitalize public belief in the monarchy and force the press into re-affirmations of loyalty. The *Evening Standard* commented: 'Mr Muggeridge may sneer as much as he likes, but the position of the throne has never been less open to challenge.'

Fleet Street was less happy, however, with the Palace press office of the time and, in particular, with its chief incumbent, Commander Richard Colville. He was accused of being obstructive and of misleading inquirers. '"It's no use ringing the Palace" is a common comment among newspapermen,' noted the *News Chronicle*. The Press Council complained in its annual report: 'The comment is sometimes heard from news editors that the Secretariat neither understands nor gives the news they want, or the necessary guidance on what is, or is not, likely to become news. The Council records this with regret, but it would be lacking in candour if it pretended that dealings between the press and the Press Department in the Royal Household were always happy or harmonious.' This was quite a smack from such a mealy-mouthed body, so it must have been sorely provoked.

Colville was certainly a stiff-backed courtier of the old school. 'Basically,' says Robert Lacey, in his book *Majesty*, 'he distrusted all the media with the guarded exception of the BBC, and he saw his principal responsibility as to keep them out of his mistress's private life. This created a deep wariness between the Press and the Palace which his successors have had to work hard to overcome.'

The office of press secretary at Buckingham Palace has a history going back almost seventy years. Before that there was a court newsman whose office began in the reign of King George III and whose function was to attend daily on the monarch and draw up lists of royal guests, which he then delivered to the offices of various newspapers. He seems to have been paid both by the Palace and the press. A full-time salaried press secretary was appointed in 1918; the job was abolished in 1931 and the work taken over by an assistant private secretary, then restored in 1944.

In 1947, the year of the Queen's wedding, a female assistant press secretary was added 'because of growing interest in the royal ladies'; there are now two assistant press secretaries (both men), plus four press officers (all women), who co-ordinate royal engagements.

They answer to Michael Shea, a brisk, no-nonsense Scotsman in his mid-forties who pulls no punches with the tabloid press over intrusions and whose straight talking is now much respected by the media. In his spare time he writes thrillers and books about the sea. His office looks after all media arrangements, including overseas tours, for the Queen and her immediate family.

Since 1959 the Queen Mother and Princess Margaret have been looked after separately by Major John Griffin, whose affection for the media is notably muted. Prince Charles is known to want separate media representation himself, but this hasn't happened yet, mainly because of complications over budgets and liaison with the press office at Buckingham Palace.

Most of the arguments between Palace and press in recent years have arisen from intrusion into the private lives of the Prince and Princess of Wales by over-zealous reporters and photographers from the tabloid press. This harassment reached a peak in 1981 when all the national newspaper editors were called to a special meeting at Buckingham Palace, the first such occasion for twenty-four years. (The previous meeting had been called by Commander Colville at the end of 1957 when stories about Prince Charles at his prep-school at Cheam had appeared in the press on sixty-eight out of eighty-eight days of his first term.) This time the target was Princess Diana, still only twenty and expecting the royal heir's first child, who was feeling 'totally beleaguered', especially by the constant presence of photographers at their home in Highgrove, Gloucestershire. Shea asked for the distinction between public engagements and private life to be observed.

That part of the meeting went very smoothly. It was afterwards, when the editors were ushered in to meet the Queen over drinks, that the fun began. A group gathered round as the Queen said how unfair it was that Princess Diana couldn't even pop into a local shop to buy some wine gums without being photographed. When Barry Askew, then editor of the *News of the World*, suggested that 'she could send a servant for the wine gums', the Queen turned on him her brightest smile: 'What a pompous man you are!'

At the next meeting of editors in March 1985, in the old billiard room at Buckingham Palace, Shea had nothing to complain about, but thought it was time for press and Palace to compare notes on what had happened since the first meeting. It was a low-key affair. Then the editors were introduced to the Prince and Princess of Wales. This time it was the turn of the *Daily Express* editor, Sir Larry Lamb, to be on the end of a royal rebuke. The Princess charged him with two false stories about her—that she had a personal rift with Princess Anne and that she had caused the resignation of the Prince's private secretary, Edward Adeane. 'If I was thirty-three this might wash off my back, but I'm only twenty-three and it hurts,' she said with some force.

The problems over Princess Diana go back to the courtship, when Fleet Street waited impatiently for Prince Charles to make up his mind, having previously linked him with a variety of other suitable and less-than-suitable consorts. Royal engagements are notoriously difficult in this respect. Those involved need privacy and time to be sure; the press wants it all in the open straightaway. The Queen managed to keep her own relationship with Prince Philip away from the press, even though they were secretly engaged for nearly a year. The newspapers never got near, mentioning only the Duke of Rutland, the Earl of Euston and Prince Regent Charles of Belgium as likely contenders for her hand (although Chips Channon had tipped the marriage in his diary).

Press speculation about the engagement of Princess Anne and Captain Mark Phillips in 1973 was expressly denied by the Palace, a fact which rankled with Fleet Street afterwards and created distrust of future denials. In fact, it isn't the habit of Buckingham Palace to issue explicit denials, no matter how shocking or untrue a story may be, but they broke that self-imposed rule on two other occasions. One was when the *Daily Express* announced across its front page: CHARLES TO MARRY ASTRID—OFFICIAL. The effect was to kill off even the first faint stirrings of romance with the Luxemburg princess; the Queen was widely believed to favour such a liaison, but the couple had barely met. The other denial followed a front-page *Sunday Mirror* story, ROYAL LOVE TRAIN, in which it was claimed that Prince Charles had been secretly meeting the then Lady Diana at night. This story provoked special annoyance, being seen as a reflection not only on the lady in question but on the honour of the royal train.

If the Palace sometimes seems paranoid about the press, it has good reason to be. Anytime Prince Charles showed interest in a member of the opposite sex, the tabloids had stalked her like wild deer. The pack was led by James Whittaker, then of the *Daily Star*, now of the *Mirror* (once billed as 'the man who knows the royals') and the *Sun*'s Harry Arnold ('the man who *really* knows the royals'). Armed with binoculars, accompanied by photographers with telescopic lenses, Whittaker and Arnold persisted in their royal duties all over the world, spending thousands of pounds chartering planes and boats. One of their tastier scoops consisted of photographs of Princess Diana wearing a bikini in the Bahamas while six months pregnant. There were unseemly scenes on the ski slopes in Liechtenstein when the Princess waved a fist at press helicopters overhead. On another occasion photographers leapt out of a hedge at Sandringham while the Queen was teaching Princess Diana to ride, provoking Prince Charles to say to them: 'May I wish you a Happy New Year—and your editors a particularly nasty one!' This is one of the few occasions when the Queen has been known to protest about an incident affecting herself. Even in this case, she was probably more concerned about the Princess's safety—and, perhaps, that of the horse.

However, even frenetic media activity about the Royal Family carries an implicit recognition of the importance of their role. For this reason, perhaps, the Palace does not condemn or deplore the coverage, but actually seems to welcome it. Their criticism is reserved for some of the methods used and for the invasions of privacy too frequently involved. They sense that it is a part of the royal function to boost public morale and entertain the people with colourful spectacle and human interest at a time of national hardship and international gloom. It can also be helpful: Princess Anne's public image was transformed not only by her work for Save the Children but by an interview she gave to Kenneth Harris of *The Observer*, widely quoted elsewhere, in which she said she would really like to be a truck-driver.

The Queen is also aware that public perceptions about the Royal Family are not created by the fantasies and rumours of the tabloid press, but through television, where people can actually see them at their work. They can see them and hear them and form their *own* impressions. Richard Cawston's famous film, showing the Queen washing up after a barbecue and Prince Philip asking if the sausages were ready, introduced fresh air and informality into royal coverage, which had been somewhat stilted in the past. The fact that Princess Diana is so remarkably photogenic has made her an international media megastar; she has injected youth and film-star glamour into a royal image that was beginning to seem rather dowdy and middle-

Princess Elizabeth's first encounter with the microphone her father dreaded so much was when she and Margaret broadcast to the children of the Empire on 13 October 1940.

In 1957, the Christmas message from Sandringham was televised for the first time. New techniques had to be learned.

aged. Overseas tours are now covered by the television companies more thoroughly than ever before because of the spectacular colour films they provide, not just for newsreels but for feature spin-offs that can often be sold abroad. The Queen's Christmas broadcast is no longer a severe unsmiling lecture, but is enlivened by events such as royal christenings, which are opened up to the television cameras back-stage rather like the footballers' dressing-room at a cup final. The effect is to humanize the Royal Family and make them seem more accessible and less forbidding. The conversation between the Queen and the late Indian Prime Minister, Indira Gandhi—for all the apoplexy it induced in the likes of Enoch Powell—illustrated, as nothing else could, her role within the wider commonwealth. It was exactly the sort of thing that Lord Altrincham had been calling for nearly thirty years before.

However, despite all this massive coverage and the Royal Family's unprecedented exposure to the media, there is a central paradox: the Queen's own mind and personality remain virtually unknown. She steadfastly refuses to be a performer. She gives no interviews. It is inconceivable that she could ever stand on a pavement, as Prince Charles did outside the hospital after the birth of his first child, and have an impromptu chat with people in front of the cameras, answering all their personal questions. It comes as a surprise to discover that journalists were invited to her father's home at 145 Piccadilly fifty years ago to hear about her menagerie of pets, which even then included several corgis and Shetland collies, two fawns, fifteen blue budgerigars and some ponies. (It is even more surprising to learn that a Post Office engineer called Albert Tippele, sent to repair the telephone at the Piccadilly house, was reported to have spanked her on the bottom for poking around in his tool bag.) The silver jubilee celebrations of 1977 seemed to cheer her greatly and she has appeared more relaxed since. She may have truly felt for the first time, as her grandfather King George V discovered at his jubilee in 1935, that the people really loved her for herself. She must also be glad that the succession is now guaranteed through two more generations.

People who have met the Queen in private all agree on the fizziness of her conversation. She can be very witty and has a gift for mimicry. None of this is evident to the public, which seems a pity. Although she must be the most photographed person in the history of the world, few photographs do her justice. Harold Macmillan wanted her to smile more in public. But she cannot bring herself to act out a part that doesn't come naturally to her. She finds it undignified to ingratiate herself in this way. She thinks people expect her to be solemn on public occasions. That was the way she was brought up to be.

She is still remarkably like the young girl described in the *Daily Telegraph*'s coronation supplement of 1953: 'She smiled but rarely, and even when she did the smile seemed at times strained. But frequently she smiled spontaneously, and then it was not her face alone but her whole aspect, her whole personality which altered.' This was the period in which the Queen's own concept of royalty was formed and the best clues to the way she sees her own role are probably still to be found in the language of the time at which she dedicated her life to public service. 'It is the happy quality of our recent rulers,' said the *Daily Telegraph* on the day of her coronation, 'that they are, in a mystic, almost a sacramental way, projections—idealizations—of ourselves: ourselves as we would wish to be. Gone is the almost deified Royalty which moved on a plane removed from reality: the Royalty of the golden staircase or the cruel caprice. The Royal Family of Britain, since the days of Queen Victoria, has mirrored in an ideal form the family of Mr Everyman. There have been, as there must be, disagreements; there have been, as there must be, crises; but the family, as a unit, stands four-square to the winds of the world.'

Queen Elizabeth has no reason to like the press. Her family have suffered from its intrusions and its vulgarity. It has angered her husband and caused her children and daughter-in-law much distress. Its pompous hypocrisy did much to destroy her sister's happiness when she might—probably should, in retrospect—have married Group Captain Peter Townsend. At the same time, the Queen cannot rule effectively without the media—they control her access to the people and condition public attitudes towards her. So far, despite many trip-wires, Queen Elizabeth has managed to preserve that careful balance between aloofness and over-familiarity.

Apparently walled in by the gentlemen and ladies of the Press, the Queen is at ease. On royal visits (as here, in Portugal, March 1985) the media escort serves the royal purpose, on the whole conveying to the rest of us the image chosen by the Palace. The printed page is less tractable.

Nothing pleases the Press more than catching the Queen off guard: taking a flying leap (far left, Turkey 1972); exposed by the desert wind (top left, 1979 tour of the Gulf States); valiantly trying to drink from a coconut (above, Polynesia, 1982); pulling faces at a garden party (top right, on the same tour); prodding the wheels of a carriage (above right, Windsor horse show); turning her binoculars on the Duke (centre left, Melbourne 1962); stamping in the divots on a polo field (left, Windsor 1955); and bending down to have a really good look at something (right) — in fact at a fishing boat in the Maldives in 1972.

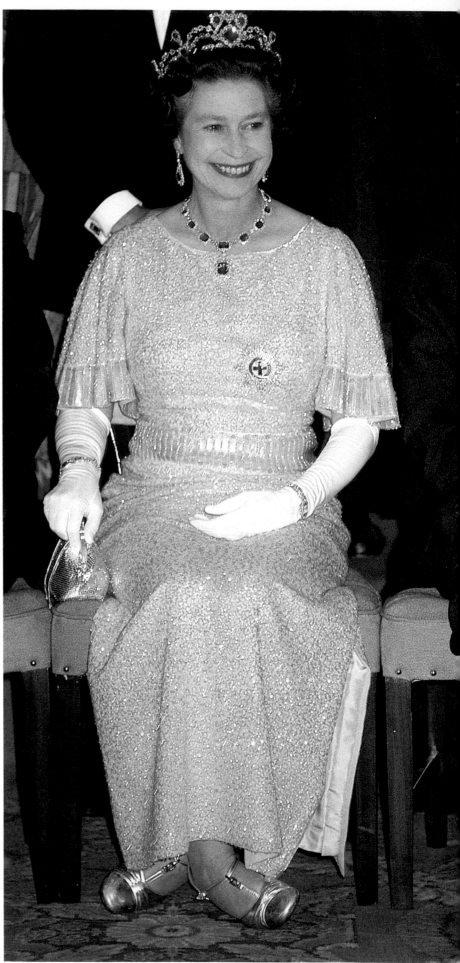

It may seem difficult to catch Her Majesty in unlikely poses, but over the years the photographers have managed quite a few: she belies her formal dress by crossing her feet like a little girl (right, August 1979); is practically speared by the bouquet of an over-anxious child (above, Wolferton, January 1985); brings the prizes out of the bag at gun dog trials (opposite page, above left, Balmoral 1973); grins under her glasses (above right, Windsor horse show); and looks askance at President Reagan and Mrs Thatcher (opposite page, below, Buckingham Palace, September 1984).

The object of a picture is often to show the Queen in an unfamiliar setting: receiving flowers from what seems like a street gang (above left, with the cast from the musical *Starlight Express*, 1985); apparently joining a religious order (above centre, National Eisteddfod, 1946); talking over a fence (above right, to her son-in-law's father); visiting a coalmine (far right, 1975); and on the tube opening the Victoria Line (right, 1969).

Ann Barr

QUEEN OF CAMOUFLAGE

The style of the Sovereign

There is nothing remotely self-conscious or 'for the camera' about the Queen. This should be a flaw. She completely lacks the instinct for presentation that most leaders and politicians have—the ability to improvise for the crowd. When Churchill met her at the foot of the aircraft steps in 1952 on her return from Kenya as queen after the death of George VI he wept. It was unfair on a woman of twenty-five who had just lost her father. But she did not break down. She had set herself to show no emotion in public.

You see the Queen Mother on television bestowing a gracious kiss on one of her grandchildren—she knows how to behave in front of the cameras. But the Queen's very awkwardness and shyness make her trusted. A king or queen is not perceived as an individual, but as the ace of a set of face cards. It might be thought that our dry-biscuit queen would have been better cast as a consort or courtier with someone more vivid as the ace. But her apparently stiff, retiring personality is actually just right for the person playing sovereign. A queen so lacking in egotism escapes all blame for any unpopular actions by Buckingham Palace, the government or her family; on the orther hand, if things go well she gets the credit.

Queen Elizabeth II does inspire loyalty and affection, unlike that stylish monarch George IV. For the Queen's style is that she has no style. But although she is not a stylish *person*, she has, by accident and training, the style a queen of a middle-aged country should have.

Personal style is something a man or woman shows consistently and noticeably. It is either ahead of the 'high style' of its time or well behind it, or it can be a deliberate use of the style of a group of contemporaries far removed from the stylist, as when Zandra Rhodes made punk dresses. It is always self-conscious.

Stylists know what they are doing and, more vehemently, what they are rejecting: style is essentially a matter of rejection. In the fifties, the stylish woman rejected cluttered clothes, wearing one good brooch and a string of pearls with clothes that were so understated that the cut and seams stood out in all their subtle detail. Unstylish women looked frumpy, lampshady and more cash than dash, more

The essentials of the Queen's style have hardly changed. The neat suit and off-the-face hat (right) could belong to any period or place (it was actually 1961 at the races in Lahore) and the outdoor gear (left, Windsor, 1975) is standard.

treasures. Buckingham Palace is an extraordinarily unstylish, 'un-decorated' house, but in every ante-room hang Rembrandts, Gainsboroughs, Friths. To select, rearrange and reject among so many marvellous things would be unthinkable. Luckily, the Queen is not even tempted to change her inherited rooms, and has not done much to make life in her palace, castles and houses modern or informal. It would disappoint people deeply if she did.

Elizabeth still has time for her dogs and horses (her seven corgis spend most of her private life with her, and sleep on her bed), and her way of recovering strength to do her public job is to spend time alone in the empty countryside of Sandringham or Balmoral. Her remoteness is an important aspect of her style. A gregarious heart-on-sleeve monarch could be a disaster—like Edward VIII.

Coming from that wartime generation brought up in an atmo-sphere of scarcity, equality and duty, she has never changed from a down-to-earth yet idealistic way of thinking. She is a democrat and *bien-pensant*, moulded by her teenage years: the years of Rab Butler's Education Act (1944), the end of the war, and the Labour general election victory of 1945. 'Too grand for the likes of us' is the Queen's reported reaction to Princess Michael of Kent. 'Grand' is the word Sloane Rangers use when a 'show-off' impinges on their world.

The Queen's dedication to her job has kept her mentally young. She has not had to compromise her ideals, or learn to act, or become a saleswoman. Politeness and goodwill have been enough. In her large family, she is thoughtful, amused and amusing, but still a bit stiff. She likes jokes, and silly family happenings. As a wife and mother she has a bit of the Lorna Doone complex—the unassertive woman who enjoys being the centre of a large clan of tough men and badly behaved animals.

Now at sixty, she seems happy and, finally, confident. She knows more about politics and world events than most politicians. She is an expert on farming and a wizard at bloodstock breeding and racing. Her taste in the arts is very average; she far prefers outdoor sports.

People read into the Queen's character what they want. She is the opposite of colourful. She is a discip-lined, natural-coloured person, not walnut cake but water biscuit. This is her strength. You don't get tired of her, and you can't exactly analyse her—she has not the predictability of the self-seeking. She will do what is required by her duty. Queen Elizabeth is a high-minded woman in a high position, with a style that is not veneer but through and through.

Princess Elizabeth's square-dancing rig in Canada in 1951 (left) was actually considered noteworthy in its day. She has been dressed in unremarkable print frocks (right, on board *Britannia*) since childhood.

Princess Elizabeth came straight out of dresses that were too childish into clothes that could have been her grandmother's (left, at Hackney children's hospital in 1947; above, with Chelsea Pensioners in 1947). After her engagement (right) she merely looked matronly. But a strapless black gown in 1952 (below) provoked much comment. She looked best in working clothes (below right, 1947).

The Queen's evening dresses are stiff, timeless backdrops for tiara, jewellery and decorations (far left, 1962, centre, above 1984). They are the clothes of an icon, a personification of majesty, and have nothing to do with fashion. Occasionally a naturalistic detail, like the fact that the Queen wears glasses for reading, fights against the formal effect (left).

When she dresses to please herself (right, in jodhpurs in 1959, left at Windsor in 1972), the Queen wears flat shoes, a kilt or tweed skirt, a headscarf and country jacket. She looks exactly like every other Sloane Ranger.

Her Majesty may lack Nancy Reagan's instinct for presentation (top left) but she doesn't look like an ancient twenty-year-old either. In the clothes chosen to suit her hosts' prejudices in Saudi Arabia (top right, 1979) she looked taller and more regal, a happy result of conforming to custom. Off guard (above) she looks like any middle-class woman who never quite mastered make-up. She looks as if she doesn't think about clothes and at her best (right, Portugal 1985) inspires affection through being unaffected.

The royal handbag has always been a nuisance (opposite page, top left, at a fete in Abergeldie in 1933). It is difficult to dispose of (opposite page, centre left), awkward to carry (opposite page, bottom left), and can hardly be hung over the arm of a throne (opposite page, right). The bag serves no useful purpose, but it was an indispensable accessory of the decently dressed woman during the Queen's formative years.

The function of the royal hat is simply to be there (above).

On duty — and that is what she is here although the photographs are designed to display her 'at home' — the Queen wears what is chosen for her, a dress to indicate afternoon neatness, jewellery to mark her function. Her outfits are like a uniform: the power of her image is that it is impersonal. We know that no woman would put on those brooches to do a jigsaw, but that is not the point. She is conforming to expectations of royalty.

Garden parties at Buckingham Palace (top left and above) are great indicators of the royal style in 'Sunday best'. The one in 1947 (far left) is a classic. Queen Elizabeth leads the way in the over-the-top clothes she has made her own. Behind stalks Queen Mary wearing the kind of tocque she was never without. The Princesses follow, Elizabeth wearing an outfit best charitably ignored, while behind her is Princess Marina of Kent, the only royal lady who could then have been called stylish. In the Eighties (left) the Queen's party outfits look nice, pretty and affordable.

Hugh McIlvanney
ALL THE QUEEN'S HORSES
────── Days at the races – and the royal stud farms──────

When two or more racehorses hurtle simultaneously across the line at Royal Ascot in one of those rare finishes that confuse even the bookmakers, one practised pair of eyes high up in the stands is likely to have identified the winner long before the camera silences the clamour of wagering with its official pronouncement. Armed with such soundness of judgement, most people on the course would be inclined to descend on the betting ring like the wolf on the fold. But in this case the expert witness is the Queen of England and, although she works noticeably hard to bring a sense of democracy to her considerable involvement with racing, getting in among the scuffling punters is never going to be part of the fun.

That she does take huge pleasure in a day at the track cannot be doubted and, if the unavoidable limitation of movement is bound to be irksome to such a natural racegoer, it can have odd compensations—not least that satisfying ability to sort out the blurred, last-stride dramas at Ascot. 'The Queen is a marvellous judge of those photo-finishes largely because she always sits in the same place,' says Lord Porchester, who has shared her deep enthusiasm for horses since they were childhood friends and has been skilfully managing her racing interests since 1969. 'If you are moving around the course, watching races from a lot of different angles, you're sure to get it wrong much of the time. However, even having a consistent vantage point wouldn't help much if she weren't basically a good reader of a race. She definitely is. I'd have to say her eye is better than my own when it comes to spotting and interpreting everything relevant that happens in running. To describe her as a real authority on practically every aspect of the game is not a courtesy, just a statement of fact.

'She likes to go racing whenever her duties permit and not only to the big occasions like the Royal Meeting or to see classics at Epsom or Newmarket. She has had a great time at places like Sandown and Newbury, Bath, Kempton, York, Doncaster and Salisbury. And, of course, she sees a lot of racing on television. She has it taped for her

From childhood the Queen has been eager to congratulate a winning horse (left, at Richmond in 1934; right, with her own horse at Ascot).

and then sits down and watches it when she comes in from a day's work. That's one of the ways in which the sport helps her to relax. It's something she can really immerse herself in, a world quite different from that she inhabits when she is fulfilling her responsibilities as the queen. I might be able to ring and say that some of the horses in training have worked extremely well on the gallops or that one of her mares has just given her a lovely colt by so-and-so. And perhaps the news distracts her from something the Prime Minister has had to tell her on a Tuesday evening or from one of those disturbing secrets that only she and very few other people in the country have to carry around in their heads. Many of the urgent official messages the Queen receives contain an element of gloom.

'It might simply be word of the death of someone who served her somewhere in the Commonwealth. She might remember the old boy with affection and be saddened to hear that he's gone. I've made her laugh by telling her that when racing people I know learn that one of theirs has completed the course they tend to say, "Oh dear, that's awful—a terrible blow. What do you fancy in the 2.30?"'

It is plainly no obstacle to the Queen's enjoyment of racing to have Henry Porchester as manager. The heir to the earldom of Carnarvon (it was his grandfather, the fifth earl, who teamed up with Howard Carter to open Tutankhamen's tomb) is a large, engagingly worldly man with sufficient energy to have built up a substantial record of public service in local government and elsewhere while running the family's beautiful 6,000 acre estate and famous stud, Highclere in Hampshire. And obviously Porchester's relations with his most famous owner are made very much more enjoyable because of her comprehensive knowledge of the Turf. He was an eager boxer all through his time at Eton and later for the Household Cavalry—an area of experience that might have provided me with a conversational escape hatch if the detailed consideration of equine bloodlines had become a shade too technical during my recent visit to Highclere. But the danger was never severe. Though my education in matters of the Turf has been expensive rather than comprehensive (leaving me some way short of mastery of thoroughbred genetics), I was made to feel almost as comfortable when discussing Hyperion as a foundation sire as I did when the subject was Sugar Ray Robinson, the daddy of all middleweights.

Astride her own pony, c.1932.

Every one of the outstanding professionals concerned with the Queen's breeding and racing operations—Michael Oswald, the manager of the royal studs, her trainers Major Dick Hern and Ian Balding, Willie Carson and all the other leading jockeys who have ridden in her purple, scarlet and gold colours—endorses Henry Porchester's assertion that nobody has to worry about baffling her with complex technicalities or insider's jargon. Carson, a pathologically ebullient Scot who spent part of his early life in a Stirling prefab, is often to be seen having animated, sometimes jocular, exchanges with Elizabeth after dismounting from one of her horses. Although Willie gives the impression that he would not remain ill at ease for long in any company, there is little doubt that he relishes reporting to an owner who knows a hock from a handsaw and a well-ridden race from the other kind.

'Perhaps it seems an inappropriate thing to say about a lady and a monarch,' Lord Porchester suggests with a smile, 'but in the context of breeding and racing the Queen is thoroughly professional. Mention any worthwhile race by name and she will know instantly where and when it is run, what the distance is and the prestige it carries. Whether you are talking about a horse's conformation or action or temperament, about the effects of particular weather on the going at a specific course, about trying to achieve hybrid vigour in breeding or the obstetric and gynaecological basics of the foaling process, you won't faze her. There is not a trace of the dilettante in her approach.'

Since the moment she sat on a Shetland pony called Peggy (a present from her father) at the age of three, the Queen has been captivated by horses. The fascination of racing and breeding reached out to her when she was taken to the Beckhampton stables of the legendary trainer Fred Darling as a teenager to visit two remarkable horses that had been leased to King George VI by the National Stud. Sun Chariot won the fillies' version of the Triple Crown (1,000 Guineas, Oaks and St Leger) in 1942 and the colt Big Game won the 2,000 Guineas in the same year. After watching these two stars work on the training gallops at Beckhampton, the future queen was allowed to pat them in their boxes. She still remembers the wonderful feeling it gave her to touch the 'satiny softness' of a thoroughbred's coat for the first time.

There was nothing satiny or soft about the tiny man who rode Sun Chariot and Big Game to those four classic wins. Gordon Richards was, in 1942, already well on his way to becoming the most successful jockey in the history of the British Turf, but it would be more than a decade before he took his only victory in the Epsom Derby. When he did, it was at the expense of the young woman who had admired his feats in her father's colours in the middle of the Second World War.

In 1953, the year of her coronation, the Queen had probably the most hopeful contender for the Derby she has ever owned, a brilliant chestnut colt called Aureole. But Aureole, having diminished his chances by sweating up in the preliminaries, was beaten into second place by Pinza, ridden by Gordon Richards. When the Queen said that disappointment over Aureole's defeat was diluted by the fact that Richards had at last claimed his Derby she was articulating a warmth she had felt for the great jockey since those girlhood days in Fred Darling's yard. Sir Gordon remembers that as he rose after being knighted by the Queen at Buckingham Palace in 1953, she said: 'I see you had a good day yesterday.' He had ridden three winners at Brighton.

Aureole, who won the King George VI and Queen Elizabeth Stakes as a four-year-old and subsequently emerged as a splendid stallion, was a grandson of Feola, a foundation mare who has done much to vindicate the Royal Family's insistence on seeking to breed rather than buy the finest racehorses. Another horse bred at the stud, Highclere, provided the Queen with perhaps the most exciting afternoon she has ever known on a racecourse when, on 16 June 1974, in the incomparable setting of Chantilly, the filly galloped home ahead of twenty-one rivals in the Prix de Diane, the French equivalent of the Oaks. The horse, whose other accomplishments included a victory in the 1,000 Guineas and second place in the King George VI and Queen Elizabeth Stakes, had been named after the Carnarvon family's stud at the suggestion of the Queen Mother.

The tribute was legitimate, considering that the filly was sired by one of the stud's resident stallions, Queen's Hussar (who also fathered the magnificent Brigadier Gerard) and had her career significantly shaped by Henry Porchester. A photograph of the royal party taken at Chantilly just as Highclere was passing the winning post shows the Queen with her hands clasped in front of her and a look of quiet exultation on her face, while off to her right the habitually elegant Lord Porchester appears to be rising in euphoric dishevelment towards the roof of the viewing stand. It was the first time the Queen had seen a horse of hers run on a French racecourse and even the locals were conspicuously happy about the outcome.

She had been accorded an equally favourable reception a few years before when she travelled to Normandy to be a guest of the Duc d'Audiffret-Pasquier at his Sassy Stud. As she journeyed through the Orne Department, weathered old men in black berets were taking the pipes from their mouths, raising fists in the air and calling out: 'Vive la Duchesse.' A member of her French escort, sorely puzzled by these salutations, turned to the Queen and said that he could not understand why the shout was not 'Vive la Reine.' 'Well,' she responded gently, remembering her antecedents, 'I suppose in a sense I am Duke of Normandy.'

Now, at the time of her sixtieth birthday, the Queen's keenness to have beautiful horses around her shows no signs of abating. In the late summer of 1985 she had twenty-seven animals in training and twenty-four brood mares, of whom only two were barren and two had not been covered. Of her twenty yearlings, eleven were fillies and nine colts, which represented a better ratio than is usually to be found at the royal studs, where there has long been a strange preponderance of female produce. 'I wish to hell the trend would change,' said Lord Porchester, reporting that there were twelve fillies to six colts among the 1985 foals. It was somewhat galling when the mating of the superb Derby winner Mill Reef with the Queen's home-bred Oaks and St Leger heroine Dunfermline resulted in a chestnut filly and Highclere's union with another Derby winner, Shirley Heights, also produced a filly.

However, satisfactions continue to outstrip let-downs in the royal thoroughbred operation, and its economic viability is not shaken by a couple of seasons in which a series of problems has caused performances on the racecourse to fall below the usual standard. The enterprise—run with the Queen's private money, never state funds—has been centred for some time on the Sandringham and Wolferton Studs in East Anglia and a third at Polhampton in Hampshire and on the racing stables of Dick Hern at West Ilsley in Berkshire and Ian Balding at Kingsclere in Hampshire. The Queen also has a substantial shareholding in the formidable sires Bustino (Wolferton) and Shirley Heights (Sandringham).

Lord Porchester's Highclere base sets him neatly between the Hern and Balding establishments but he says it is far more important that both yards are reasonably convenient for the Queen when she is at Windsor or even in London. Just as she delights in helping to decide upon the best matings for her breeding stock and in arrving at ingeniously apposite names for the offspring, so she thinks nothing of rising at six at Windsor Castle in order to be out on the downs to see the first horses exercising at West Ilsley an hour-and-a-half later.

The Queen will travel much farther than that to scrutinize distinguished horseflesh. Since attractive pairings for her powerful harem of brood mares are inevitably difficult to contrive in this country she naturally looked forward to visiting the Kentucky studs whose stallions have had such a profound impact on the world's bloodlines in recent decades. And when she did make it to the bluegrass pastures in 1984 the trip was soon surpassing all her expectations. Not only was she able to arrange to have some of her best mares covered by coveted stallions (Highclere by Nureyev, for example) but the sheer joy of being in such genuine horse country prompted her to declare that she was having one of the very best weeks of her life.

But then, in the middle of an American night, tense telephone calls began to come through from London. The IRA had bombed the Brighton hotel where Margaret Thatcher and senior Conservative colleagues were staying for the annual party conference.

The Queen immerses herself in her favourite world every time she has the chance. She knows well enough that sooner rather than later she will be hauled back to the harsher place in which modern monarchs go to work.

All the best jockeys have sported the Queen's colours: Willie Carson, Epsom 1977, on Dunfermline.

A British royal who was not mad about horses would be regarded as a bit of an oddity. No such fears were entertained about Elizabeth.

On her tenth birthday she displayed her splendid seat in Windsor Great Park (opposite page, above left). Eleven years later she and her sister cantered along Bonza Beach, East London, South Africa (opposite page, above right); and in June 1956 she took her children to Windsor to see their father play polo (left). But she is not to be outfaced by a mere horse (right).

Prince Edward shares his mother's jubilation at her win (left), but no sympathy is shown to losers, not even husbands (above left, Windsor 1976). The Queen turns out in all weathers, trudging through mud to present the prizes at Windsor (above right) and braving an impending storm to join her mother and sister in the back of a cart, the better to survey the field (above, far right, Badminton 1977). Right, a conference which appears to hold little interest for Margaret.

A day at the races demands concentration (above), especially for the Queen and her mother who are owners as well as enthusiasts. The Queen can be found in the midst of the throng at Ascot (right) or at the winning post at the Derby (opposite page, above, Sir Gordon Richards winning his first Derby in 1953). Her first Classic win, in 1957 with Carrozza ridden by Lester Piggott, was a proud moment (centre). At Royal Ascot each year she drives down the course in the state carriage drawn by four greys (opposite page, below right).

The whole brief drama of a race is reflected in their faces as the Queen and Lord Porchester watch Shirley Heights win the Derby at Epsom in 1978. Top, left to right: exhortation gives way to anxiety and then dismay, followed by (bottom, left to right) jubilation, triumph and congratulation.

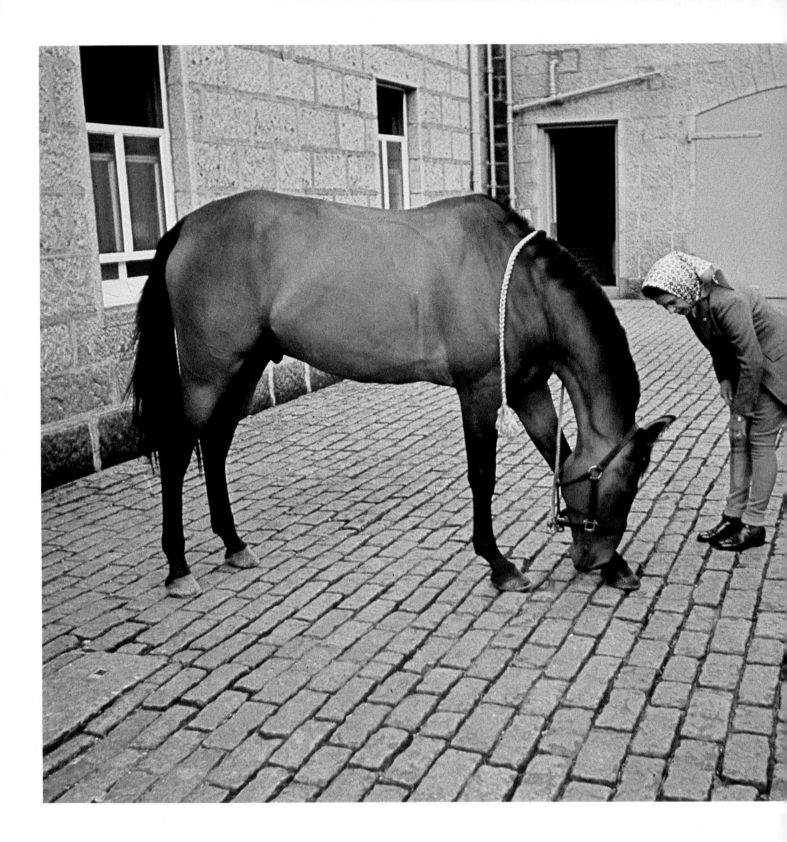

Among the many
photographs taken to
celebrate the Queen's
silver wedding anniversary
in 1972, it was only fitting
that some should reflect
her enduring love of
horses. Patrick Lichfield
captured her concern in
the stables (above) and
her enjoyment in the park
at Balmoral (right). It's
appropriate too that the
Queen's official birthday
should find her on
horseback. She is always
at her best at the annual
Trooping the Colour
(above right, 1984),
showing her skill and
control over her mount in
1981 when a disturbed
young man shot a pistol
loaded with blanks near
her in Horse Guards
Parade. After the
ceremony, the horse is
always the first to be
thanked (far right, in 1972
with Prince Edward).

Clancy Sigal
AMERICA'S FAVOURITE SOAP
—————————A transatlantic view of the Royal Family—————————

There is Royalty, and royalty. No American boy of my generation, no matter how patriotically drenched in 1776 War of Independence iconography, could possibly escape infection by the English royal bug. The Jewish and East European immigrants who were producing the Hollywood movies which influenced us so strongly may have escaped their own kings and czars, but they shrewdly understood the American hunger for the undemocratic glamour of Bette Davis's Elizabeth I, Madeline Carroll's Queen of Zenda, Katharine Hepburn's Mary Queen of Scots and other studio-made queens forever knighting Errol Flynn or Ronald Colman on their broad shoulders. There was an element of reality too; genuine affection in our Chicago working-class neighbourhood for Edward Prince of Wales when he mingled with the unemployed Rhondda miners and demanded 'Something must be done.' When the Prince, as King Edward VIII, abdicated 'for the woman I love'—lucky American girl!—the hardest anti-British hearts softened. It was like an Ernst Lubitsch film, if without his saving touch of irony.

Chicago was rough turf for British royalty. From top to bottom the city was run by an Irish political mafia whose front man, Mayor Big Bill Thompson, had made an election promise to punch King George V on the nose if he ever came to Chicago. There were votes in this anti-royal bluster. But also bitter memories of the Great War when, it was popularly held, the wily British had schemed to drag American boys over to die on the European fire. For years Chicago's most powerful newspaper, the *Tribune*, was edited by Colonel Robert R. McCormick whose mad anti-British bile once produced banner headlines, in the middle of World War II, exposing a Whitehall plot to invade the USA—through Canada. Such was the Midwest's isolationist temper, not everybody laughed at this scoop.

But it was the 1940–41 Blitz—Princesses Lilibet and Margaret Rose, gas masks askew, sheltering like other Londoners from Nazi bombs—that set American attitudes to royalty. The pre-war monarchy was a wooden, unsympathetic institution, remote as King George, severe as Queen Mary. The war humanized British royalty, turning them from an untouchable monarchy into an imperilled family. American war guilt played its part too: stammering, shy Bertie and his brave wife were in the front line against fascism while most of us were relatively safe and prosperous. By 1945 a whole genera-

George Washington
stretches out an
admonitory hand in
Wall Street, New
York, June 1976.

tion was hooked on Princess Elizabeth's favourite colour (yellow), on Margaret's quirky smile—on a royal family that, while legitimizing its own class pyramid, also legitimized in some odd alchemical way the democratic, patriotic, institution of the American family.

Historically, we Americans kicked the royal habit 200 years ago—which isn't to say we don't have vague hungers in that direction. Wallis Simpson never quite made it, and after all Grace Kelly ruled only a toy-town principality. Were we trying with the Kennedys to create a home-grown royalty? Briefly J.F.K. had the glamour of a young king and Jackie his debutante queen; they induced in normally sceptical, even radical, citizens the same effect of glazed wonder that traditionally the Queen has on Labour ministers. But assassination and revelation shattered the fragile illusion.

The Royal Family seems to be an extraordinarily necessary cultural form in which all of us work out our innermost fantasies. This is as true of Americans and foreigners, especially if they live in England, as it is of most Britons. The Royal Family exists on the far side of our psyches as well as in front of our eyes. They're plugged into us, and vice versa, on a level of intimacy some families never achieve in real life. They suffer for us; are braver than us; have more luxury and leisure as by right. And when all about them is breaking up, they stick together—despite Group Captain Peter Townsend and SS fathers and divorce and rumours of separation and hints of Royal affairs—as if God gave them a special cement denied the rest of us.

It is a truism that the British Royal Family is television's first monarchy. Queen Elizabeth's reign was born at the same time the new medium was introduced to Britain; in a sense, television and the Royal Family have grown up together. The monarchy has adapted splendidly to the television age with each royal member, no matter how distant, playing a quite specific role. It's like an electronic *commedia del arte* and goes to the roots of popular drama: there's the

Jackie Kennedy with children John and Caroline and brothers-in-law Robert and Edward at Runnymede for the inauguration of the Kennedy memorial stone on 14 May 1965.

serene-but-horse-playing old mum, the good-but-troubled older son, his fairy princess, the randy young brother, the sad sister, the glamorous-but-grasping social climber and so on. It's pure soap opera—and everybody knows it. *Dallas* and *Dynasty* are quite conscious pale copies of the original. And like the prime-time soaps, the Royal Family revolves around a plot that's also a hymn to the extended family, and to the getting and keeping of vast wealth.

I'm not sure that my fellow Americans make that big a distinction between *Dallas*, *Dynasty* and the Royal Family. As tourists they flock to Buckingham Palace as to a London version of South Fork. They mean no disrespect; indeed there is some awe at being at the source of a television super-drama. They gush and enthuse and fall over themselves with admiration and envy—which is not a bad way also to describe Fleet Street's attitude to the royals.

But what uninvolved, Stateside Americans have described to me as a mere 'camp fairy tale', or 'a slightly daft version of "Upstairs, Downstairs"', or 'the ultimate fantasy of aggrandizement' or 'like an appendix, a hangover from a bygone age' is taken more seriously by Americans on British soil, depending on how long we've been here. It has to do with how much of the British package you buy on arrival. One reason why expat Yanks tend to be firm, if slightly shy royalists is the shock of realizing that no matter how hard we try we will never be British. Most of us really do want to *belong*. The Uncle Toms acquire a phony English accent, pseudo-county mannerisms, join a club and do what we can to stifle our natural vulgarity. (Yes, I had this phase, mercifully long past.) The rest of us miss, among other things, the quintessentially American habit of giving one another awards. Prizes and banquets for service, humanity, charity or just for staying alive past forty are as American as Coca Cola. And of course in Britain the only generally respected source of awards is the Queen: gongs, knighthoods and orders may be bought and sold as cynical political favours, but Her Majesty's monopoly of bestowing honours inevitably magnetizes us towards her.

On the face of it the Royal Family is not exactly promising raw material for fantasy. Until recently there were no great physical beauties (gawky Di has grown into one, but Princess Alexandra, my personal pin-up, is not to everyone's taste). Intellectual brilliance, well. There is a tendency, Randy Andy aside, to chinless wonders. Their only talent, indeed pleasure, seems to be riding horses and shooting things, preferably alive and furry. And yet, some years ago, at about the time the Home Office gave me permission to stay indefinitely, I began having the most persuasive pro-royal dreams. The Queen invites me to tea and says she secretly admires my writing. Princess Margaret and I hail the same taxi on a rainy night in Fulham Road and end up at her place not mine. And, repeatedly, in almost every conceivable circumstance, I save the Queen's life from

the bullet of a crazed assassin. And of course receive a 'gong' from her own hand at Buckingham Palace.

To my relief, I've found that similar dreams are fairly common among Americans who live here, including radical republicans and feminists. One feminist who dislikes Princess Diana at a rational level—'she's set women back several years with that young perfect mother image'—has confessed she can't read enough about Di in the women's magazines and frequently dreams of saving Prince William from death. Another friend, one of the staunchest left-wingers I know, gave me a hard-line analysis of socialist fears of royal political intervention, and then grinned awkwardly: 'But if you put me on a couch I'd admit that Prince Charles's interviews before his wedding and just after the Toxteth and Brixton riots, and when he denounced Peter Palumbo's modernist plan to vandalize London's Mansion House area, tapped a great secret yearning I have for a prince–king with the common touch, however counter-revolutionary that sounds.'

We resident Americans, like many Britons, are terribly possessive of the Royal Family. Constitutionally, they may not be ours, but they get into our blood. But our love for them is not without a touch of sadism which we pick up from the natives or maybe from the down-market press. (See, for example, the *Sun, Mirror* or *Daily Star*'s handling of Diana's post-natal 'neurotic anorexia' or the hints about her bossy way of sacking old retainers.)

Regularly press and public run the gamut from a kind of voracious love and admiration through bitchiness to equally whole-hearted pity. Americans often tell me they feel 'sorry' for the royal plumed birds in their golden cage of ritual exhibitionism. And the more serious books about the Royal Family consistently suggest that most of them were emotionally deprived children. They're something be-

In the States in 1976 for the independence bicentenary the Queen stretches out a hand to a jazz trombonist.

tween sacrificial victims in the traditional religious sense and Holly-wood super-stars who are victims of the very publicity that sustains them.

To enter the world of royalty via its true consecrators, the media, is to leave this world and its troubled logic not for fairyland but royal-land: a Disney-esque leisure complex with its own logic, rules and pleasures (and no doubt pains). The Queen and her entourage arc practised exponents of the moves, gestures and dialogue conducive to the so-called religious trance that is supposed to strike those who meet them in the flesh. The essential thing is for royalty to act out in public what for any normal person would be a grinding contradiction: to be superhuman with a common touch, knowledgeable without being moved by such knowledge, to be goading Fleet Street into its worst excesses while snarling at the intrusion on royal privacy. The Royal Family is permanently and gladly married to the media; it could hardly exist without the press to fight with and pose for.

The Queen is like a great actress, sincere in all her roles, devout in the narcissism necessary for her sanctity. Americans and other foreigners who long for a true aristocracy and look down their noses at the Queen as a middle-class frump completely overlook her almost impeccable sense of stagecraft. She is producer, director and main star of the royal pageant, a kind of repertory classic which, in between jubilees and royal weddings, has to work hard to hold its audience. The Queen's unthreatening dowdiness is a calculated, even inspired, masterstroke of theatricality: the ordinary made majestic, mystical.

Even the lesser royals collude brilliantly with their media stereotypes. American policemen I know come to behave like Clint Eastwood's Dirty Harry and criminals learn to swagger like Al Pacino in

'The Godfather'; so too, the members of the Royal Family acquire a skill in playing with, or to, the roles assigned them. Like any stars they may find it easier to go with the deluge of personal publicity than to assert an individuality that is never really encouraged in the first place. Of course, the roles change and develop, and with them the royal players: Diana from fairy princess into radiant mother and regally compassionate but 'with-it' wife; Andrew from bumptious brat to lusty playboy to war hero; Charles from polo player to mystic vegetarian to beef-eating social activist. It's crucial, of course, that there be some fallings-off—and not just from polo ponies: Prince Andrew's romp with Koo and others, for instance, the Duke of Edinburgh's fits of bad temper, or Princess Margaret burning the candle at both ends.

It is also in the nature of pop culture families, from the Ewings to the Carringtons to the Windsors, that the actors be re-consecrated from time to time by appearing as their 'true' selves in the mass media. Hence Princess Margaret on 'Desert Island Discs', Princess Michael on the verge of tears on Breakfast Television, and—most remarkable of all—the transformation on the 'Terry Wogan Show' (where else?) of Princess Anne from surly grouch to mature mateyness. Somehow the aura of royalty is enhanced rather than diminished by this adaptation of its medieval mystique to the global media.

The Royal Family is soap opera but with a political function: survival of 'the firm' and anything that helps renew its licence to rule. I have a feeling that if there were a socialist revolution tomorrow in Britain somehow the royals would adapt and find some way not only to hang on but to maintain themselves as models of revolutionary decorum and stability. Ultimately, the most interesting thing about them is that they are not Romanovs but a hardier, less romantic, and more sensible breed.

I remember precisely when I fell out of love with the British Royal Family and stopped having dreams of wrestling their would-be assassins to the ground in single combat in Pall Mall. One night I was sitting in an audience at the Dorchester Hotel ballroom entranced by a performance Marlene Dietrich had just given. One of the royals was sitting at a nearby table. A well known but 'tired and emotional' actress wobbled shakily over to attempt a curtsy. The actress was American, and I completely understood her spontaneous attempt to pay her form of tribute to British hospitality and all the other graces that keep us here but are hard to put into words. Inadvertently the actress touched the royal presence as she nearly fell down in her effusive, inelegant bow. I will never forget how chillingly, killingly, the affronted royal personage froze that poor drunken woman with a stare that would have petrified an SAS man. That may be 'Royal' behaviour but it isn't very royal.

On the steps of the Pentagon in 1976 (top left), the British Queen helps the United States celebrate its liberation from British rule. Six years later she welcomes President Reagan and Nancy to Windsor (top right) and rides out with Ronnie (right).

Clive James

HOWDY MA'AM
─────How the Queen wowed the West─────

When the Queen and Prince Philip visited California in 1983 it was the tour that had everything: Royalty *and* Hollywood, 'Palace' meets 'Dallas'. The only problem was that the West Coast's famous sunshine was eclipsed by the extravaganza. Down came the deluge and up went the umbrellas. They called the Queen the rained-on monarch. Undaunted, *The Observer* sent one of its best men, Clive James, author, wit and caption-writer extraordinary, to dog the royal footsteps. He even stayed in the same hotel as the Queen, just along the corridor and only 27 floors below. From this position of intimacy he developed the close rapport with his sovereign which is revealed in this photo feature.

Modelling rainwear for a *Playboy* advertising spread at the Rancho el Cielo, the Royals look regal and the Reagans look reagal. The Queen and the First Lady show two different

approaches to the basic mackintosh and boots. While Nancy rashly defies the elements from the neck up, the itinerant monarch has sensibly added protective headgear.

Meanwhile the President addresses the nation concerning the economic upturn which, if it continues, will enable him to throw away that piece of string and buy a tie.

During 'The Star-Spangled Banner' the Queen stands waiting patiently to hear the familiar strains of her own song. The President, who has grown an additional right arm since taking office, salutes with the upper arm while using his lower hand to indicate the position of a small nuclear-powered pacemaker installed in order to pump fresh pigmentation to his hair follicles.

Laughing at a funny story that one of the friars at the Mission Impossible has just told her about his bad eyesight, the Queen offers the assembled media a good shot of her famous handbag, containing the keys to the palace, all the major credit cards including the rare American Express solid emerald Fabergé card which enables her to cash up to $1000 worth of traveller's cheques a day, and a powerful short-wave radio for listening to the racing results in England.

Assigned to the Queen for her one-on-one protection was Captain Roscoe S. Kilroy of the crack Combined Special Services underwater skydiving unit, the Black Moustaches. This is the way he looks before he starts getting dressed. Scanning the rooftops for any signs of encroaching frogmen, Roscoe could check the credentials of British photographers in the dark. The Queen was heard to say, 'Knowing that Captain Kilroy was only one step away at all times was a great comfort to me, and to my husband.'

At a lunch hosted by Los Angeles Mayor Thomas Bradley. President Ronald Reagan dematerializes, leaving an empty chair which is gazed at in astonishment by the visiting Queen and her consort. At the very moment he vanished in Los Angeles, the President appeared in Washington and told Congress that the economic recovery would be endangered if the investigation of the EPA were to continue. He then returned to Los Angeles for coffee and liqueurs.

In the reception line, Perry Como passes away on his feet and is held upright only by his hair transplant, but there is still time for Nancy Reagan to save Frank Sinatra with mouth-to-mouth resuscitation. George Burns, still bitter about English perfidy during the War of Independence, in which he fought, ignores the Duke of Edinburgh's proffered hand. Ed McMahon, Johnny Carson's straight-man, cries 'Here's Johnny!' to relieve the tension, although since Carson was at home with toothache the stratagem was only partly successful.

Up on the roof of the Santa Barbara College of Jellybean Technology, one SWAT squad has just spotted another. Jellybeans are very important to the President, who tends to favour an ice-cream flavoured variety called McConnell's Jelly-Bellies, the formula for which was developed at SBCJT. A packet of mixed Jelly Bellies, of a suitable size to be carried in a handbag, was formally presented to the Queen as a souvenir for Prince William.

At the San Diego zoo, Prince Philip is shown a koala bear and asks 'How long have you been a koala bear?' He went on to compliment the bear's handler, Celeste Heisskumpf, on the beauty of the city of Sydney, saying that he and the Queen were delighted to be there again. Interviewed later on CBS news, the koala said: 'I think Bagehot's arguments for constitutional monarchy are pretty hard to answer, even though I have to admit I'm a Bob Hawke bear myself. The Duke's got a nice, firm, dry handshake.'

At the Royal reception dinner at 20th Century-Fox in Hollywood, Rod and Alana Stewart arrived incognito. Hoping to escape attention in his black leather suit, Rod gave the game away when he accidentally stepped in a pot of molten gold on the way out of his strong-room after counting his money. Rod and Alana now share not only the same hairdresser, but the same hairdryer, a novel double-headed apparatus which can be winched down on them while they sit in the whirlpool bath casting each other's horoscope.

Visiting Sutter's Fort, a township still populated by traditionally dressed descendants of the pioneers, the Queen wears mourning because all her other clothes are sopping wet from the torrential rain. *The Observer* is only now able exclusively to reveal that the pioneer walking a step behind Her Majesty is once again the resourceful Captain Roscoe S. Kilroy of the Black Moustaches, this time cunningly disguised. The lady on the right, Mother McReegan, a distant relative of the President, is quietly choking on a home-baked chocolate-chip cookie.

At the Sacramento Sunset Home for Davey Crockett look-alikes, two long-term residents die from happiness at the Queen's visit and are laid out for the vultures by their fellows, who sing a specially composed verse of the heroic woodman's ballad: 'Born on a table-top in Tennessee/Kilt by a smile from the monarch-ee'.

The President, who was once considered for several plum roles only to see them go to Humphrey Bogart, takes his revenge by saying 'Here's looking at you, kid' to the Queen. Her Majesty, who thought he had said 'Here's looking at Euclid,' replied that geometry had always been a puzzle to her at school. Thus in an atmosphere of mutual understanding the tour became a legend.

Finally the Royal Couple flew home to Britain in the Space Shuttle, with the Duke at the controls. 'You see, darling,' he told the Queen, 'the Yanks have got these things very cleverly worked out so that all you have to do is pull the odd switch just to keep the computer happy.' The Queen's face spoke volumes about her confidence as the Royal Scuba Tour of the Americas came to an end.

Colin Cross

TOURS DE FORCE

————The Queen and her travels————

As head of a commonwealth of forty-nine nations, Queen Elizabeth II has the widest sphere of influence of any person on Earth, considerably larger than that of the Pope. Of course the direct authority of the Queen has dwindled to vanishing point and she has none of the Pope's executive power. But there is no doubt that one of the distinguishing marks of Elizabeth II's reign has been her determination to make a reality of the title of Head of the Commonwealth. Certainly some predecessors of hers would not have bothered very much. After all the Commonwealth is the ghost of the old British Empire and can easily be dismissed, as Voltaire mocked the Holy Roman Empire for being 'neither holy, nor Roman, nor an Empire'. Voltairians who tried to use that kind of language about the Commonwealth in Elizabeth's presence would get short shrift.

There is no mystery about how Elizabeth has brought the head of the Commonwealth role to life. Queen Victoria could sit in seclusion as Kipling's 'widow of Windsor' and be admired—and romanticized—by her subjects across the world. She, of course, was the apex of imperial authority and every British official exercised power in her name; a modern 'widow of Windsor' would fare badly with the people of the Commonwealth and it is only by going out herself on her incessant tours and visits and seeing the people that Elizabeth II can make an impression. It is almost like an American election candidate needing to win votes by shaking as many people's hands as possible—except that the Queen is purveying influence rather than seeking power. The aim is nothing less than to promote human understanding, to provide a common focal point that works for many different nations.

It is air travel that has shaped the Queen's modern Commonwealth role. When her grandfather George V made his one voyage to India in 1911, the journey took him three weeks each way and involved a suspension of all ordinary routine; he was the only British king-emperor of India ever to attempt such a thing. Elizabeth II flies around the world as regularly as many international business executives and must have clocked up a larger mileage than any other head of state.

The Queen's journeys are planned to eliminate nearly all jet-lag. Everything is organized in advance; she never goes anywhere in a hurry. Typically, a trip is decided two years ahead and the outline planning is complete about a year before it takes place. She has

'Come fly with me' (left): the state visit to France, May 1972. A more leisurely way of wafting through the air (right) in Tuvalu in the South Pacific, 1982.

developed a keen eye for a schedule and the danger spots in it which could cause overstrain. There is a convention that Elizabeth does not attend funerals and this helps cut down any rush. Whereas a prime minister may have to drop everything to fly off to a funeral in Moscow or New Delhi or wherever, the Queen quite simply never goes. (The only public funeral she has attended, other than those of members of the Royal Family, was that of Sir Winston Churchill.) And this convention fits in well with the head of the Commonwealth role; to decide which Commonwealth statesmen and women should merit her presence at their obsequies would impose impossible problems of protocol. The result is that Elizabeth has succeeded to an astonishing degree in making herself a mistress of jet travel rather than a slave to it. Not as a royal 'miracle' does she nearly always manage to look fresh and smiling wherever she happens to pop up in the world.

The *Britannia* is a vital adjunct. The Queen rarely sails in the royal yacht on a long ocean voyage. The pattern is for the vessel to sail on ahead of her and she flies out to join it at the destination. The *Britannia* gives her a combined hotel and office, a floating base from which she can operate in familiar surroundings and dispense hospitality. The 5,000-ton yacht, which cost £2·1 million to build in 1954 and had an £8·6 million refit in 1980, is part of the Royal Navy and requires a crew of twenty-one officers and 256 ratings; the running costs are around £3 million a year. In the early years of the Queen's reign when *Britannia* was new, there was a good deal of public criticism about it, as if the ship were some kind of pleasure cruiser. The Admiralty used to issue careful explanations of how it could be converted into a hospital ship in case of war. However, it has long been plain that *Britannia* plays a central part in the Queen's working life; it is one bit of the Commonwealth that the British Exchequer finances with no help from any other member-country. As a matter of fact, the yacht is none too comfortable for a stormy ocean voyage, despite various stabilizers having been fitted; the Queen has quite a line in sea-sickness jokes. She was forced to move ashore to a hotel during the 1983 California visit, the sea being too rough for comfortable cruising in *Britannia*.

Up to the end of 1984 the Queen had carried out forty-seven official overseas tours, mostly to Commonwealth countries; she has visited every member-country at least once. This figure does not include private visits, of which there have not in fact been very many: unlike Victoria, Elizabeth does not make a habit of adopting a pseudonym ('Countess of Fife') and taking holidays in such places as Cannes. All this travelling can be quite a hardship for her at times, especially in tropical climates: the Queen suffers from sinus trouble, which is aggravated by sun, and the refuge in her own familiar quarters in *Britannia* can be vital. As the long reign continues the frequency of visits has actually increased, from one or two a year to two or three. Her attitude is far more relaxed than at the time she came to the throne when she would read out stilted speeches as if half-paralysed with nerves. Today the speeches are still read but she sounds thoroughly at home with the texts; she is more like a politician who employs a speechwriter for the raw material than a pupil reciting a lesson.

Tour etiquette is much the same anywhere. The Queen will don special garb, such as a black veil for the Pope or long sleeves for the King of Saudi Arabia, but in general the only workable method is for people to adapt themselves to her. In republican countries women are not expected to curtsy to her, although many do so. The bow for men is a slight inclination of the head which would be a routine courtesy for any significant person.

One key rule is that the Queen must not be taken by surprise. The lists of those to be presented to her are prepared in advance and gate-crashing is a high social crime. 'If you find you are to be presented to the Queen,' advised the *Los Angeles Times* during the 1983 California visit, 'do not rush up to her. She will eventually be brought around to you, like a dessert trolley at a good restaurant.' In principle, one should never take the initiative in conversation with the Queen but leave it to her to decide what topic to raise. She will respond with some such formula as 'How interesting'—and generally sound as if she means it. Those who break the rule and raise a topic of their own are likely to be answered with a dismissive 'Oh, really?' This should not be counted as arrogance or stuffiness so much as simple caution. Everything the British queen says is followed with avid newspaper attention; she simply cannot afford impromptu remarks. And over the past thirty-four years she has carried on conversations with an estimated 150,000 individual people.

Ever since the Duke of Windsor, when prince of Wales, had his right hand crippled through too much handshaking in Australia in the 1920s and had to wear a sling, the Royal Family have avoided too much hand-to-hand contact. When the Queen does shake hands, she uses a special 'royal grip' by which she grasps only the tip of the other person's fingers. Handkissing is definitely out, except as a formal pledge of allegiance from someone accepting office—then the subject kisses the air immediately above the Queen's hand and not the hand itself. It is gross *lèse-majesté* to reach out and touch the sovereign; the Canadian provincial premier who, in 1984, tried to guide Elizabeth by grasping her elbow received a frosty reception. It was probably surprise as much as anger which brought such a look of apparent fury to the Queen's face, clearly caught in photographs. When her face slips from its customary affable, smiling pose, it is generally because she has been taken unawares. It may even be something that has amused her and she is suppressing a laugh.

Elizabeth's tours had begun by the time she succeeded to the

Soon after the Coronation, in November 1953 the Queen and the Duke set off on a Commonwealth tour in the liner *Gothic*. The route included London, Jamaica, Fiji (right), Tonga, New Zealand, Australia, (left, leaving Sydney for Tasmania), Ceylon, Aden, Uganda, Libya, Malta, Gibraltar.

throne. George VI, who had wanted to tour the Commonwealth, had been prevented from doing so by ill-health and the then Princess Elizabeth, with the Duke of Edinburgh, set off in his place in 1952 towards Australia and New Zealand. She had got only as far as Kenya before the King's sudden death.

Almost as soon as the coronation was over in 1953, the Queen and the Duke set off on a long 173-day tour in the liner *Gothic* (in which she became the first reigning monarch ever to circumnavigate the globe). Elizabeth took her coronation robe (but not her crown) with her to wear at parliamentary state openings. The voyage took them across the Atlantic to Bermuda and Jamaica then over the Pacific to Fiji, Tonga, New Zealand, Australia and Sri Lanka (then called Ceylon). 'Thank you very much, Sir Walter Raleigh,' said the Queen to Mayor Buttle of Auckland when he covered her with an umbrella during a shower of rain. Altogether, it was computed, the Queen made 102 speeches and shook hands with 13,213 people. The voyage finished off in the Mediterranean with calls not only at Malta and Gibraltar but also at Libya, then temporarily a British protectorate. In fact it was at Tobruk that the Queen first set foot in the newly-completed *Britannia*, which had sailed out with the young Prince Charles and Princess Anne aboard. The return home was such an event that the City of London gave a formal banquet of welcome in Guildhall. Since then royal returns to Britain have become too routine to rate Guildhall feasts.

In the following years the royal couple went to Norway, Sweden, Portugal and Denmark. In 1956 there were three weeks in Nigeria—the first trip carried out entirely by air—and in 1957 the Queen aroused polite applause in Paris for her British clothes designed by Norman Hartnell. Later the same year came the first of the North American visits, with the coronation robe donned again for the opening of the Canadian parliament in Ottawa. Also in Canada the Queen made her solo debut on television. Then she was with President Eisenhower in Washington before moving up to New York to make a brief address to the United Nations. She was back in Canada in 1959 for the opening of the St Lawrence Seaway—*Britannia*'s masts were fitted with hinges so that it could sail under the bridges.

The early 1960s was the peak time for the liberation of the former British colonial empire, especially in Africa. The Queen herself never attended the formal independence ceremonies, although she always sent a member of her family to represent her. She did, however, make a point of visiting fairly soon afterwards.

Dr Kwame Nkrumah of Ghana actually became the first of her prime ministers—before Harold Macmillan—to know that the Queen had become pregnant with Prince Andrew, when she had to postpone a planned visit to Ghana. This visit did take place two years later, but it was against a background of public disorder, which included bomb threats, and there was talk of London taking responsibility for the Queen's personal security. But the position remained that in

Ghanaian affairs she acted entirely on Ghanaian ministerial advice. The area of who, exactly, is responsible for the Queen's security outside Britain remains a grey one. The Ghana visit itself went off peacefully, however, although there were some gaps at the state banquet due to last-minute arrests of some of the guests.

The touring has continued ever since, with visits to several Commonwealth countries each year, and sometimes to non-Commonwealth ones. The Queen opened Sydney Opera House in 1973 and wore spectacles for the first time in public when opening the Canadian parliament in 1977. In 1983 she made a major tour of India, during which she awarded her personal order of merit to Mother Teresa of Calcutta and appeared in a television dialogue with the late Prime Minister Indira Gandhi. There was an important foreign visit to Germany in 1965, renewing old family links which had been broken for over half a century. There have been two further major American visits. It was not necessarily monarchical countries which knew how to treat the British Queen with the most courtesy; in 1980 the King of Morocco kept Elizabeth waiting in a tent in the baking desert while he himself sat in an air-conditioned caravan. Some of the British entourage advocated cutting the tour short but the Queen went on to entertain him to dinner in *Britannia* with what was described as 'frigid courtesy'.

Following a dangerous visit to Jordan in 1984—dangerous not through ineptitude by King Hussein, who ranks as an old friend, but through bomb attacks on him—the Queen accepted in principle an invitation to tour Israel. This will fill one of the last remaining holes on the world map on which the two biggest gaps are, of course, the Soviet Union and China. On present form China looks as if it will be the first to be covered. The idea of the Queen going to the Soviet Union has been mooted for twenty years—and the Duke of Edinburgh has been there in his World Wildlife capacity—but there are still obstacles. Had the Bolshevik revolutionaries executed merely the last Tsar it could be taken as part of politics, but the Yekaterinburg massacre of Nicholas and his entire family still casts a shadow.

At sixty, Elizabeth II is still going at full steam and tours by the dozen must lie ahead. That she will add to her amazing collection of experiences by one day walking into Lenin's tomb in Moscow's Red Square, Soviet officials bowing politely around her, cannot be excluded. After all she did attend the US bicentenary celebrations—and she told the Americans she more or less agreed with what they had done in 1776.

The royal yacht *Britannia* (top, in Tuvalu, 1982), launched in 1953, has travelled over 600,000 miles. There are periodic rumblings in the Commons about the expense. A hefty amount of luggage has to be stowed on board (bottom left), as well as a train of attendants (centre in Kiribati 1982 with — from left to right — doctor, lady in waiting, equerry, press secretary wearing dark glasses). The Queen's Rolls is well kitted out (bottom right) with clock and storage for tapes of military music.

Arriving gracefully is a key part of royal procedure and sometimes circumstances conspire to create the perfect entrance. On the visit to India in January 1961 (above) all went well when the Queen stepped down from a carriage in Delhi. Sometimes, however, the elements are less than kind. In Muscat, Oman, in 1979 (far right) protocol demanded that Sultan Qaboos remain rigidly to attention during the anthem while the Queen struggled with her hat in the wind. Rain never stops play. From the Coronation onwards, many a big day has produced a downpour (sequence of photographs right, returning from Jordan in 1984).

Welcomes come in many guises (above). Large crowds are commonplace but the sheer mass of cheering people in Australia in 1963 (left) was extraordinary. Detroit's fire boat put on a magnificent display for Princess Elizabeth in 1951 (top) when she was on her way to Canada.

Travelling is not all
protocol; there are many
occasions when the Queen
clearly enjoys herself. At
the races in Bahrain in
February 1979 (above
left), she and the Amir
discussed the field in
comfort. In Tonga in
February 1977 (left) she
was amused by the banana
leaves. King Taufa'hau of
Tonga must be the world's
heaviest monarch (right):
he tips the scales at over
28 stone. It's hard to
imagine what the Queen
and a Soloman Islands
chieftain found to talk
about in October 1982
(above). The European
monarchs (top) at the
D-Day anniversary in
Normandy in 1984 were
more familiar company –
many are relations.

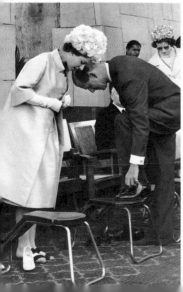

Early in 1961, the Queen made her first visit to India, though the Duke had been there before. They laid a wreath on Gandhi's tomb, taking their shoes off first (far left), renewed acquaintance with Mr Nehru (left), and the Queen addressed her largest-ever audience in Delhi (above). In 1983 she met Mother Teresa in Delhi (centre left) and the redoubtable Mrs Gandhi (top left) shared the Queen's Christmas broadcast.

Times change, and so do royal tours. No trip today would include a tiger hunt (above, Rajasthan, far right, Nepal, both 1961). But in Nepal Prince Philip did not shoot: his trigger finger was diplomatically bandaged. Shooting with the camera (right, in Nepal in 1961) is quite acceptable. The royal couple almost always get the opportunity to visit the most spectacular sites the host country can offer – by now they must have seen everything this side of the Great Wall (top, in Africa, 1965). The tiny South Pacific island of Tuvalu (overleaf) is a welcome change from more complex countries.

The 1979 tour of the Gulf states produced lavish displays of hospitality. In Oman (above), the red carpet treatment was literal. Not to be outdone, Sheikh Abdullah Jabir of Kuwait indulged the joint passion of the royal houses with a day at the races (top right). The trip to Morocco in 1980, however, was a disaster. King Hassan, a monarch with a strong sense of his own importance, frequently kept the Queen waiting (above right) and changed the order of events at will. Afterwards there were questions about the purpose of the visit. Had trade with Morocco been worth it?

Who meets the Queen used to be a matter for hours of anxious debate. From the start children were an automatic choice. Like the Brownies in Basutoland (top left) on her southern African tour with her parents in 1947. Children on a beach were a feature of the visit to Japan (bottom left) during the Far East tour of 1975.

People are dressed up in ceremonial costumes which now lack all menace (centre left, Maori 'warriors' in New Zealand 1977). But during the 1977 New Zealand tour a new concept was introduced, the walkabout. Henceforth the Queen would mingle with the crowds and talk to people who interested her (above).

Education and the army are staple ingredients in the diet served up to the Queen on her tours. She can never visit too many schools (overleaf, Portugal in March 1985) or review too many troops (right, also Portugal). Religion is quite another matter. An audience with the Pope at the Vatican in 1980 (above) was more controversial: the Queen is head of the Church of England after all. Her tiara and decorations also emphasized that she is head of state.

The 'Her Majesty
shares a joke' cliché
seems for once to be
true on walkabout in
Antigua.

Simon Hoggart
CARIBBEAN QUEEN
The 1985 royal tour of the West Indies

As with her birthdays, the Queen's official arrival and her actual arrival are two different things. So it was some hours after the royal yacht *Britannia* had docked at Bridgetown Harbour, Barbados, that the motorcade of dignitaries drew up at the quayside and the guard of honour formed ranks. A band played 'Life on the Ocean Wave'. The guard, members of the Barbados Defence Force, wore green uniforms with snappy yellow cravats, so that they looked a little like subalterns at a stag night.

Then the Queen stepped out on to the gangplank. As often happens, the local police had got it into their heads that their job was to keep the press as far away as possible. This is a mistake. These days Buckingham Palace occasionally even asks journalists, in a discreet sort of way, to cover the Queen's tours, to make up slightly for the imbalance in interest between Her Majesty and her daughter-in-law.

The police tactics had been honed and refined during the visit of Ronald Reagan in 1982, when security was so strict that almost nobody set eyes on him. He went even the shortest distances by helicopter, so that the locals called him 'our friend in the sky'. In the event, while policemen with swagger sticks pushed us around, a chap strolled casually through the guard and saluted a few feet from the Queen. When they picked him up he explained that he had wanted to bring her the good news about God.

Next she inspected the guard. It isn't much of an inspection, really. She walks briskly past them as if they were a bus queue, shooting a sideways glance or two. She certainly hasn't got time to shout, 'That webbing is filthy. What's your name, soldier?'

The first stop was at the new Central Bank building. It wasn't exciting, but the Queen is expected to show an interest in what her hosts are proud of rather than in what she might enjoy. She must often be gripped by the despairing boredom said to afflict pioneering Intourist travellers visiting another new tractor factory. After unveiling a plaque she went on a walkabout, in the rain. She looked a little tense and made a beeline for the few white faces, carrying her special see-through umbrella. 'Are you all on holiday?' she asked, several times. Then the sheer enthusiasm and delight of the Barbadians seemed to touch a sudden chord. 'Queen, God bless you,' someone shouted. 'Lovely woman, man,' said someone else.

At the Barbados Museum she met Miss Billie Miller, who is education minister—a job of some prestige here where the literacy rate is 97 per cent. Soon afterwards Miss Miller became involved in a heated argument with a youth who wished to know why the Government was spending a reputed quarter-million Barbados dollars (around £90,000) on the 48-hour visit. 'Because she is queen of Barbados', Miss Miller told him sharply. 'Barbadians are very hospitable, especially to the Queen.'

Later she added, a touch ruefully, that since independence the younger people no longer shared this feeling. At school, she had learned only British history. The mystique of the monarchy must suffer as the Tudor kings disappear from tropical textbooks.

Le tout Barbados was at the garden party that afternoon. There was music, exotic drinks and people slithering in the mud—a sort of Woodstock for monarchists. The main social event was to be the official dinner on board *Britannia* in the evening, but the guest list for that was short and ordained by protocol. Not being invited to the garden party was a far more wounding snub. People had been preparing for months. Some had flown to Miami, 1,600 miles away, to get their outfits. The invitations stipulated hats and white gloves, so near panic set in when the Bridgetown shops ran out of gloves. Happily a shipment arrived from Britain at the last moment. In such ways does the Empire still support home trade.

As in London, the Queen is steered carefully round selected guests for brief conversations. She has three basic expressions, on which all others are variations: a dour glare verging on a scowl, delight, and lively interest. It is the last she uses at garden parties. Some people take it for a genuine desire to learn all there is to know on the subject in hand. Thirty-odd years of experience have taught her how to cope. She simply walks away—then turns and flashes a brilliant smile from a few feet adrift. Short of yelling, 'Come back, I haven't finished yet', there is nothing they can do and no way they can feel hurt.

The royal yacht is her preferred means of travel, since it allows her, we are told, to return hospitality wherever she goes. In fact, this simply means local worthies troughing twice at the expense of different taxpayers. Dinner is served on Minton china and there is a separate service for dessert. This is in green and 22-carat gold, so that each plate is worth several hundred pounds. Stewards are encouraged not to drop them. There are five monogrammed wine glasses at each place setting. At formal dinners, the Queen generally wears a tiara. Around the walls are gifts from various rich foreigners, including a pair of camels under date palms given by a Middle-Eastern potentate. The piece is of solid gold and the dates are made from rubies. It is stupendously vulgar, and so what? People want royalty to be over-the-top.

The food is as good as can be coaxed out of a tiny, broiling-hot galley. Custom insists that nobody continues eating after HM has stopped. This used to leave slow eaters hungry and sometimes resentful. These days she pushes her last few peas around the plate until everyone else is finished, a serviceable metaphor for a constitutional monarchy. She has smaller cutlery than the guests, using a dessert knife and fork for the main course. There is no loyal toast, and guests may light up when the ashtrays arrive. Afterwards there are more drinks at a short, less formal reception. It doesn't last long. The Queen is not a hostess who presses people to linger for a final nightcap. Afterwards she returns to her private quarters at the stern of the ship, and the other 318 people on board—who include a 26-piece marine band—go to their more cramped accommodation.

Next morning dawned hot and bright. The sun sparkled on the silver beaches. A cooling breeze raised whitecaps on the sea and swayed the fronds of the coconut palms. So what could be better than a visit to a cement works? Away we bowled, past ranks of waving sugar cane and schoolchildren. So wide has the fame of Fleet Street spread that the children's cheers for our bus were extremely loud and even more sarcastic. We waved back, graciously.

By the time she arrived, plant management, the tourist board, Buckingham Palace staff and the police were locked in combat over who could push the hacks around most, and where. In the control room someone screamed, 'There are too many of you here.' As we fled gratefully, someone else shouted, 'Too many of you are leaving.' The Queen heard the disquisition on the manufacture of cement (necessarily theoretical, since the plant was out of order) with a polite lack of interest. As she climbed back into the royal Roller I noticed that she took the sopping wet see-through umbrella and tucked it between herself and Prince Philip. Even queens get drips on their stockings. I also noticed one of the bossy policemen accidentally catch HM's equerry, Miss Florence Gittings, a sharp and painful smack across the spectacles with his swagger stick.

That afternoon there was yet another youth rally. She has youth rallies the way we have snooker tournaments. It always seems to be time for another one. The rehearsals, we learned, had been a shambles, yet something—perhaps the massed willpower of the parents—made it work. The final performance was a dance in which young women flung up their dresses and revealed their knickers. The men in the royal box, including the Duke, beamed and clapped. Uniformed cub scouts leaped up and down to get a glimpse. The Queen employed her dour look. To most of the 11,000 children there, her role must seem a remote constitutional abstraction. She swiftly made it more tangible by announcing a school holiday. They cheered wildly. Then Their Majesties left the stadium, waving from an open Land-Rover like a pair of department-store Santas. The whole scene could have occurred, unchanged, thirty years ago.

Next we went on to Grenada, where the Queen planned to remind the Americans just who is head of state around here. In fact there

are very few Americans left—just an unusually large embassy and 500 medical students, famously rescued by President Reagan in 1983. It must be a pleasant life for them: four years' study on a tropical island followed by a lifetime playing golf.

The Queen opened the Grenada Parliament, which is where Maurice Bishop and his cronies used to hold dances and play table tennis. The British restored it to mark the return to democracy. It is functional rather than grand, like a Holiday Inn executive suite. The 'Westminster model' has been exported to some strange places, but few more curious than this tiny and sensationally beautiful speck in the Caribbean. Men with maces arrived, by-passing the modern security metal check. A chap in a wig asked, 'Is it your pleasure, Honourable Members, that the Houses do now adjourn during pleasure . . .?', using the same formula which is still heard in the House of Lords. There were fanfares, a cry of 'Order, order' from the Sergeant-at-Arms, and the Queen of Grenada climbed up to her throne, a comfy padded armchair. Even the speech contained all the clichés of home: 'eliminating the fiscal gap . . . accelerating diversification . . . agro-industries an important sub-sector . . . no easy options.' One wondered if these speeches are run up in a factory near London, like the bank-notes. Outside it began to rain again.

It was still raining in Tobago, two days later. We waited for her in Scarborough, the shantytown which serves as its capital. Mr Norman Parkinson, the celebrated photographer known to the Royal Family as Parks, was waiting with his wife and son, drinking 'Carib' beer out of the bottle. Mr Parkinson went to lunch with the Queen wearing a suit and a striped tie over a Hawaiian shirt open to the waist. This is what you can do when you live in the tropics and have been to a very good school.

Before lunch the Queen visited the Tobago House of Assembly to unveil yet another plaque, a ceremony described in the text of the chairman's speech thus: 'You have most graciously consented to unveil a plague.' She said how pleased she was to be there and pulled the little curtains. It was a pity, I reflected, that Tobago did not have a bi-cameral legislature, then she could have announced 'A plaque on both your houses'. Later there were more steel bands, then a flight back to Trinidad and another dinner on the yacht. With his inborn upper-class dress sense, Parks packed his DJ for this event.

Next day she left on a chartered British Airways Tristar. The rules insist that a two-hour gap is left around her flight when no other planes may take off or land. Somehow this fact had escaped the attention of Eastern Airways' booking office so I found my flight cancelled and myself stranded in one of the Commonwealth's less interesting airports. Even in these enlightened days, I reflected, the Queen has the means to make life tricky for some of her subjects.

After opening Grenada's parliament – to show the Americans just who is boss here – the Queen went on to Tobago's House of Assembly (left) for the obligatory plaque unveiling.

ACKNOWLEDGEMENTS

The publishers have gathered together the illustrations from the sources listed below:

The following illustrations are reproduced by gracious permission of Her Majesty the Queen

20 cl, bl, br; 30 bl; 31 t, c; 35 (photo Marcus Adams); 39 (photo Cecil Beaton); 52 tl; 130.

ALPHA-Agence Angeli 167 t, c, b; Jim Bennett 10 b; 86; 87 tl, tr; 91 t; 93; David Parker 90 l

Associated Press 64 br, 80 b

BBC Hulton 26 t; 38 tl, br, tr, cr; 41 bl, br; 52 tl; 63 t; 75 tr; 98 l; Marcus Adams half-title; 36 l; Studio Lisa 25; 34, 52–53; 70 b; 75 b; Serge Lemoine 108; 138 b

Camera Press–20 tr, c; 54; 109; 119; Baron 74 bl; Cecil Beaton 20–1 t, b; 47; 69; Tom Blau 21 tc; Andrew Davidson 107 br; Karsh of Ottawa 20 tc; Patrick Lichfield 70 t; 73; 113; 142–3; 143 bl; Norman Parkinson 89 c; Snowdon, 87 b, 94; Studio Lisa 29, 77 t; Dorothy Wilding 115 bl.

Lionel Cherruault 15; 58 tl; 100–101; 104 l; 117 t; 121; 182–3.

Colorific! Denis Brack Black Star 154 t; 155 c; 157 b; David Levenson 120 b; © 1983 Dilip Mehita, Contact 172 c.

Gerry Cranham 133.

Daily Telegraph Colour Library-Djukanovic 84 tr.

Francis Dias–19 bl; 56–7; 57 tr; 79 tr; 151 b.

John Frost Newspaper Collection 42 b; 94; 95.

Tim Graham Contents page; 78 tl, br; 78–9; 105 tr; 123 tl, tc; 129; 136–7 t; 152 l, 152–3; 153 t, b; 154–5 b; 155 t, c; 156 t; 157 t; 159; 165 t, c, br; 170 t; 171 t; 176–7; 178–9.

Anwar Hussein 21 tr; 55 br; 79 c; 85 l; 103 cr; 117 br; 118 bl; 120 tr; 126 b; 129 l; 136–7 b; 148; 149; 151 tl; 165 bl; 167 r; 170 b; 171 c; 180 c; 180–1; 182 b.

Illustrated London News 38 bl; 122 t; Marcus Adams 36 br.

London Express News Service 63 b; 67; 81; 102; 103 tl; 122 c, r; 135; 138 t.

Observer Library Baron 74 t; Cecil Beaton 80 t; Camera Press; Snowdon 77 bl; Fox Photos 43; Lajos Lederer 20; David Montgomery 124; 125; Dorothy Wilding 115 tr.

Desmond O'Neill 89 b.

Robert Opie Collection-photo: David Cripps 8; 22–3; 44–5.

Photo Source 9 tl, tr, 82–3; Central Press 42 tl; 75 tl; 139 b; Fox 32 tl; 32–3; 36 bl; 36–7; 40 t; 172–3; 174 c, b; Fox Keystone 21 c; 44 c; 49; 57 b; 58–9; 105 tl; 107 bl; 162; 169 t; Keystone 32 bl; 42 tr; 53 bc, 139 t.

Photographers International 19 b; 78 bl; 143 t; 184–5; 191; Jayne Fincher 78 tr; Terry Fincher 19 t; 179 t; 190

Popperfoto 26 b; 40 b; 44 tl, bl; 105 b; 112; 114; 115 tl, br; 134 tl; 166; 172 br, bl; 180 t.

Press Association 9 b; 30 t, br; 46; 77 br; 82 b; 106–7; 134 b, 143 b.

Rex Features 24 t; 31 l; 52–3; 91 tr; 106 l; 136 bl; 186/7.

Rex-SIPA 107 tr.

John Scott-Front & Back cover; 10 t; 19 br; 55 tr; 56 tl; 82 t, c; 84 tl; 104 r; 117 bl; 137 tr; 139 br; 180 bl.

John Shelley 103 tc, tr; 120 tl; 123 tr; 172 t.

SIPA Press, Paris 158, 169 br, 174 t.

Spitting Image 21 br.

Frank Spooner-GAMMA 145, 179 b.

Sport & General 76, 84 b, 98r.

Stare 151 tr.

Stern, Hamburg 89 t.

Syndication International 18; 61 r; 64 bl; 91 b; 103 cl, bl, br; 116; 122 bl; 140–1; 168–9; 171 b.

Times Newspapers Ltd. Mark Ellidge 136 tl.

Topham 41 tl, tr, cl, cr; 44–5; 55 tl, r; 64 tl, tr, cl, cr; 71; 74 br; 126 bl, c; 134 tr; 146; 163.

Patrick Ward 60–61; 126–7; 127 r.